FALLING

FINE

FALLING

BY MATT HART

SELECTED
& NEW
POEMS

FINE

Pickpocket Books
Bloomington, Indiana

FIRST EDITION, November 2024

ISBN-10: 0-9993985-8-6
ISBN-13: 978-0-9993985-8-6
Library of Congress Control Number: 2024946508

Cover & title page design by Rose Zinnia
Interior layout by Eric Appleby

Pickpocket Books is an imprint of Ledge Mule Press

www.ledgmulepress.org

CONTENTS

WOLF FACE (2010)

LIGHT-HEADED (2010)

SERMONS AND LECTURES BOTH
BLANK AND RELENTLESS (2012)

DEBACLE DEBACLE (2013)

RADIANT ACTION (2016)

RADIANT COMPANION (2016)

BLUE JAY SLAYER (2017)

EVERYTHING BREAKING/
FOR GOOD (2019)

THE OBLITERATIONS (2019)

FAMILIAR (2022)

NEW POEMS (2024)

Acknowledgments

About the Author

FALLING

FINE

*Hark, dumbass, the error is not to fall but to fall
from no height. Don't fall off a curb, fall off a cliff.*

—Dean Young

The obvious analogy is with music.

—Lyn Hejinian

WHO'S WHO VIVID

(2006)

COMPLETELY BY ACCIDENT

I was in a fix.

I was sloshing with joy.

I was looking at my feet and my feet looked good.

I said to my apartment, "I am a tiger. I am an iron,"
then cleared my throat and hollered, "Yahtzee!"
into the jungle.

No vapors intervened to banish the quiet from my soul.
And nobody looked in the mailbox either.

I have always understood nothing as a series of zeroes
and imagine the clouds as if I myself were a cloud,
as the hiss of a slow-leaking tire requires.

No one delivered the ice that I ordered,
No one controlled my remote from the forest.

Where was my pet rock when I needed her the most?

My little retriever with a stone in her bladder.

From the myths of beginnings to possible worlds,
I have often been wrong about philosophy in public.

When I boiled this evening's lobster this morning,

I screamed and invented a monster.

IN THE GLOAMING

I was standing I was standing up.

I was picking my way through a puddle of *awk!*

I was well aware of the uneaten green beans
and they were well aware of my well-meaning intentions.

My mission: To save the most the best-dressed for dessert,
to assert myself in the gloaming, while wondering about gloaming
and looking it up and feeling all the while tangential.

I can barely see in this light
the new puppy named Daisy.

I am not much in the way of understanding
the things I do or why that loaf of bread and not
this one with the sunflower seeds overwhelming.

Slip me the truth in a worn-out roller coaster.

Give me a sound I can make with one cricket.

I've come to fix the sink. I've been freaking over a flower.

I thought my head was half its age.

The tide washes in/ washes out.

HOW I KNOW I'M STILL MISSING

Sometimes the gladiolas backfire in my face.

I get headaches for days when I read in the dark.

When I cross the bridge at midnight
I pretend I'm a sparrow escaping a star.

Escape is not something I ever take lightly.

Behind me is a light with a lampshade most grave.

I lay my eggs neatly in the crest of a wave
and tell them to wait there until I get home.
Sometimes they listen, sometimes they don't.

I open a door and pass through an elephant,
my hair full of dust and the shadows of bells.

Someone points out a large hole in my pocket.

On the teeter-totter I feel like a million bucks.

WHO'S WHO VIVID IN THE MOONLIGHT IN PAIN

Who's who vivid in the moonlight in pain,
    too late I uncovered the nothing above me.
        Now jumping for joy in the muck overwhelming,
        singing inside me for all that I'm worth

        (and with death to keep me honest),
        I walketh the stairs with my brother King Kong,
        as alphabet blocks spill out of my pocket
        and spell not much—no particular world. Hooray!

        to discover at last: nothing's my fault,
        and what's more there's nothing to help it
    get clean. Enamored, then enchanted, but in the morning
I'm a shoe lace. And in the afternoon, I'm the building's

        unbuilding, the butcher, a sweater of man
in the bluing. Goddamn it, my darling, everyday
    I come to you conflicted, and I'm sorry. I kiss you
    on the fire escape, out into the yard. How

uncomfortable to be comfortable, to be churning
    with poems, to be messed-up and messy,
        exuberant-green... Anymore what I mean
        is like new, wet cement.
        I speak and I'm stuck in it forever.

DADA'S SAWED-OFF
HALF BROTHER

Take any line. Cut it off.
Take any new line, set it
to music, set it ablaze.
Watch it collapse into settle and haze
and forget about vision. Instead be prepared
to appear as applesauce. Be prepared
to tell us why you waltz. Cut it off at the
Boy Scout motto. Add the phrase,
To turn red, as in hot communista,
as in delicious suspect, as in
laundromat heaven. Cut off everything
before the word laundromat and everything
after the la of laundromat. Now sing
La Fortunato in the gutter. Now sing
Why are all the radicals crying?
Answer: Because they've lost their
shells of chocolate cool, their
yard-long tongues of provocative dust.
Make a line, if you will, a cut
in the dust. Let go of everything
but the whistle. Make it
wistful, make somebody sigh.
Make a mask out of oranges
and scare with it. Make cry.
Use extreme caution with amputation.

Cut up and modified, one gets amplified
and putative. One begins to break. Generous
association reveals, A needle exists.
Amplify the needle, then cut it
to pieces. Am punctured, living fury.
Therefore, need lemons. My heart won't
stop crowing at the crack of dawn.
My voice won't stop cracking at the sight
of blood. O beautiful for spacious. Cut off.

CALM POEM

Of all the calm poems I've written
this calm poem

is definitely my favorite.
It came at the end of a calamitous day—

I couldn't remember what to say
during a lecture.

I cried while reading
a philosophical preface.

When I looked in the mirror
I saw pieces of a blue jay

and the world turned
my stomach

in the gathering dust.
Forget it, said the poem.

Now you're safe at home.
Many people love you.

No need to create a scene.
No need to punctuate

the roar of the page.
Go to sleep and dream

you're a giant paper snowflake.
There is nothing to be afraid of.

HAILSTORM

An agony afoot, I burst into peacocks,
Reverdy all afternoon. Loss for loss,

nothing is easy. In one poem a horse
jumps flatly over a hedge of sparks,

the horseman blue. And a bone or a flower
is clouded with silence, everything engulfed

in the peripheral. Somehow this produces in me
pain, an unquenchable line of amputees.

As far as the eye can see them
they are walking into the sea. Yesterday,

Saturday, totally scarecrow, empty as a January
ice cream parlor, I wondered how to say

complicated in a less complicated way, how
to say abstraction and mean something actual.

And I thought of calling you, or writing a letter,
but I've been masquerading lately as a barrel

of monkeys presented all at once from every
angle. Life is a beautiful hailstorm, which is kind

of forlorn and scenic all at the same time. Or put
another way I am an out-of-work oboe player.

I wonder if anyone other than you
can detect my sincerity? And I wonder, too,

when I leave a party, is everyone relieved
that the snowflake was only a terrible dream,

do they return to their drinking and summer?
I knew I would miss you, and I do.

WHAT'S INSIDE A GIRAFFE?

Elevators going up.

The guts and black stuff of three in the morning.

An interminable list of romantic O's.

The sigh at the end of a night-long dream.

Unexpected, excellent, sausage!

Factory churning full-tilt over the wall.

Definitely Negative Capability.

Certainly the first limousine.

Echoes and re-echoes, Echoes and re-echoes, Echoes and
   re-echoes...

Narcissus.

Mommy, I'm thirsty.

Somebody give me a beer.

Evening caught in a parasol weeping.

Nerval out walking his lobster on a leash.

Rooftops.

Postmarks.

Two kids making-out in a bottomless pit.

All day, Saturday, staring at the sea.

An expert on bees on his deathbed buzzing.

The rockets, their red glaring error included.

What is is.

A pack of wild dogs.

The collected equations of Benjamin Péret.

Youssou N'Dour, Salif Keita, Oliver Mtukudzi, King Sunny Ade.

What a circus ought to be.

A song of sadness in an elephant box.

The ends of the earth.

Saliva for miles.

The exuberance missing in today's ice cream.

The hottest band in the world.

Cannoli filled with orange/bay leaf marzipan cheese, then
dipped in chocolate and served on a plate of tropical fruit
and sprinkled with powdered sugar.

The taste of raw oysters.

The shadow of Guillaume Apollinaire.

Conjunction junction, its function besides.

Cats in the hallway screaming their lives.

Information arranged in columns and sorted by zip code.

She loves me, she loves me not, endlessly.

Who you calling whitey?

Trickle down economics.

The crabgrass amazed.

The canary in its office smacking into glass.

Things are looking up, are they not?

Welcome to gravity's impossible party.

Philosophical investigations.

How about a walnut the size of a brain?.

How about an accordion that never shuts up?

Nothing comes immediately to mind, and then it just sits there.

A big, fat liver.

Polyester stuffing and an air-powered squeak toy.

What used to be a tugboat is now a digested life preserver.

O clogged gutters will you ever come clean?

Distracted by exercise, charmed by fools, the windmills.

I blush to think of it.

Feed the dog. Take a shower. Eat breakfast.

Pop goes the weasel.

Bananas and toast and a sundae with nuts.

Babble.

Rubble.

Toil and trouble.

The unraveling of X, the poems hot 'n' heavy.

The afternoon flying a jet through your hair.

Absolutely everything, even dust.

Where "I" is most certainly somebody else, what have you in
the way of identity politics?

Not Brian Vanaski.

Not a really colorful tattoo.

More procrastination than I know how to use effectively.

The hallowed halls of bureaucracy.

Spelling "estuary" correctly.

A cure for esophageal cancer.

The proper method for modeling a turtleneck.

The distance from here to your mother in spots.

From there to your father in shredded coconut.

Why pregnancy isn't an option.

If you stand on your toes, you can just make out the mountains.

A brand new Uncle Wiggly.

Survey says...

Splendiferous evening on front porch swinging.

Swallows falling out of the very worst trees.

Toy box. Solar system. Fertilizer spreader.

Time for the 7th inning stretch.

Ball of string.

Vertical tight rope.

A distant cough.

Somebody's bread and butter.

The punctum.

Whereas it used to be required knowledge for getting into
heaven, now it's only a suggestion.

Eucalyptus, Mentholyptus, Citrus.

That's a wrap.

Let's meet back here in five minutes.

I'm still in need of a cotton ball, an SOS pad, and a picture of a
lawnmower from the SEARS catalogue, Winter, 1975.

Duck-duck-goose.

Rock-Paper-Scissors.

Who put the bop in the bop-sha-bop-sha-bop, who put the ram
in the ram-a-lama-ding-dong?

Also, who wrote the book of love?

Who died trying?

With the big, ugly voice of Ethel Merman.

They saved Hitler's cock.

Incredibly powerful gag reflex.

Poor Geppetto.

The end of tap dancing.

Abecedarian.

Smooth sailing.

Rapidly approaching, a cherry blossom!

Long goodbye.

African Queen.

Size does matter, doesn't it?

A new kind of not-maple syrup.

Door prizes ranging from 1-1000 dollars.

Where the inside ends and the outside begins—that is most
    definitely the mystery.

It is written in mud, it is written on the fly.

Wild Dobby Gibson, burgled by dusk.

Strawberry fields forever.

Breaking apart on the outskirts of space.

Anything by John Cage.

Anything involving the use of a hammer.

Anything by John Cage involving the use of a hammer.

Idi Amin.

Your family having dinner.

The contents of the giraffe's stomach—primarily leaves.

YOU ARE MIST

(2009)

YOU ARE MIST

for Merrill Feitell and in memory of Paul Otremba

and your absence is company and a company.

The police once a month do the cardiac arrest,
and the mayor throws his best pitch into the shrubbery.

It's funny that no one considers the dogwood's
early blossoms, as clearly they're an indication's

indication: all ghosts long for greener pastures
in the future. Richlier burn, ye florescence,
says the drugstore clerk, forgetting he's repeating

the great city pent. Meanwhile, my hair turns
to chalk dust, and the twenty-years-younger fall asleep
over coffee. You might say the world has an air

of lime-tree bower, of balloon sure to burst
or coughing up ducks. Now near the lawn chair

by the downtown loft my prison, I am lonely
in my reaching for bewilderment's
orange emptiness, almost and only

of the me I used to witness. There is nothing there is.
And by this you mean something specific.
You mean you are missed, but I hear you are mist—

the crux of our great misunderstanding

CENTO CORSO I

Long live man!

God how I love!

Splashed across the world's loveliest floor
I am bleeding
I am coughing
Agamemnon!

Heavy like the seas
CRASHBOOM and billows of orange

But who will take the message
And who will thank the bees

Who will will and who won't will in spite

The sky is brown
The leaves are leaves
It's Spring again and Man is the victory of life

CENTO CORSO V

Dawn is sky sky is blue blue is long and far
And now for the wooly hike back to the city

Light winged light O wonder of light!
I too weep in rain at night
I can't face the stiff blanche day

Experiment and technique   Fossilific trees...

I! I! out of you, Gregory Corso

And the stars in the sky are still boss

from TOO HEAVY FOR LIFTOFF

kite string   coterie
he gladly flies the face of
gladly the ocean with buckets, he drinks of
and bruises that don't open up in the violet
or keep to themselves in electric
the swamp kiss   O swamp kiss
amplifier   stacks of guitars
we follow the tabloid's lead through the chorus
ferocious dear asparagus   most shocking
the wigwam   send money urgently
this volume's allergic
and the chlorophylled meadow,
though deepened with tourniquet,
is high as a lingerie modeling takeoff

*

camouflage camouflage,
                    disaster of soufflé
if the newspapers say grace
how do you say it butter?
if ether   if platypus
every dented note
a little bit cherry stem

the warier the kitty cat
nobody likes an ode to fashion
ever since fierceness gobbled a closeness
see I too can make a sentence too heavy for lift off
a random thing with fire ants, plaid and plaid
and played to death
granny smith's green apple tartlet with gravity
full-frontal nakedry
jaws of jaws

*

    fructose periplum caveat with bubbly
my my miraculous, the worry the worry
couldn't you just tie a slipknot
the whale feels better after vomiting the prophet
so many eponymous Weezer discs repeating
all speaking at once and contradictory to the teachings
of Aristotle, logically, of course,
the apocalypse present
now nearing the finish line firing squad airbag
seven dopey dwarves
the shepherdess covering her flock with a blankey
no wonder the field commander in the field
of wildflowers is cancelling   infinity squared in infinity's
frosting   opening a bakery is difficult work

*

you may think you'd like to dance a monster
but your gluestick's rather sticky
or rather, rather tacky, rather
six-pack buffet   but three befuddled cheers later
upon a peanut butter sandwich
you're tossed to the lake like a deadhead
from Olympus   if only you'd
been dipped in chocolate first
nobody better than a stay-at-home lightning bolt
fish don't pay attention to sculpture
any more than right now you're paying homage
to a denotation's slide whistle
if you want to be a tricycle, then you'll have to make
some changes

                    this meter's checked until 6PM,
                    Mon.–Sat.

*

patiently the snowboy
considers his galoshes   two paper bags
how we used to pack lunch   so much little
makes sense of your adoption

33

so the new rules in effect are a means
for thwarting pirates   huh?
I have my best ideas
when I'm reminding myself of yourself
in the bathtub   steam rising up
off a hot apple crisp   after a long day
of playing in the fish beneath the frozen lake
what could be better
than a head wrapped in igloo
I haven't used one euphemism

                         AC/DC

                         *

counting   no counting
no sentence of money
no money of acquisition
no acquisition of status
no status updating of status and meth
the heart is still beating   but how
and where that happens is a mystery at best
where's Matt
                         and what could he possibly think
he's proving   and to whom
in the clutter of the worms' whitest light
often the rock quarry   the robots'
sticky hatred of anything

approximating dumb humanism's
gruel   I love gruel
I will make a lot of it

*

           pile up and pile on
        the footballs are plenty
the levees are holding their breath
once in the future slash no future
on the cross-stitched horizon
I made a potholder with a lobster
impressed the hell out of Saturn,
and thus the trade of rings   sarcastically
to the shareholders who got the raw end
of the yellow fin   the middle finger
I placed in the yard is still standing,
my line in the sand still crawling
with crickets   the leopards
in my facelift   the scolding
better uncle   no uncle uncle uncle
                  unto your nervous
                  your sheepshank exploded
                  explode—

*

easy to doozy to wander no discipline
some people seem to think
and others simply abandon ship
while she's crying   I could never do that
because I'm curious about breakfast
and murmurs under covers   how
there is nothing to eat me in the sea
that I would not also eat
given the right circumstances
and a mouth with many teeth
returning to the surface
and whirling like a derelict,
the hook in my lip
like the stripes of a zebra
I flap my arms wildly and hope

WOLF FACE

(2010)

NEW DAY RISING

Bathing in purple, we are bathing in O.
The violets are brewing. We are jaundiced
incredibly. Wet to our gill slits.
An American anthem. We are human beings.

Sing it, We are human beings. Soap suds soap suds,
bath of green sailboats. Hard rock slab of chocolate
cake. And here is a smear of blood O. On the floor,

a smear of blood. In it we are bathing. A dog's white
house. The dots of trees. Cartoon loon or mouse-
trapped hole. You think you know us? You know
a bed sheet. Heaven awaits the righteous.

We are not righteous. We aren't even
warm. Come out come out whoever you are.
We promise not to eat you. We promise, but

we are liars. We lie because we are human. Because
we can and we must. We are washing our hands.
We are washing our hands O. Battery acid. The set
of our eardrums. It's dawn, and the low baby's crying.

NEW-FANGLED AIR

Whippoorwills whipping   This language isn't anywhere
Not even the rocket ship   And yet, it's morning

after weeks of partly cloudy skies and beating myself
and everybody up into submission   One, one, and one

of my commonest themes   Now peeling an orange, the world
seems easy   And later mowing the grass, being bitten

on the horse by a fly, all seems fallen apart, already
passed away, but perhaps also regenerating—earthworm halved

in two white dwarves   I look in the sky   I imagine drawing
figures in a meat processing facility, dragging myself to a spot

on the floor   The marks I make, unbeknownst to me,
funny-strange and irrelevantly weeping   Maybe

you know yourself similarly, or maybe I'm leaping
to conclusions in the dark   In any case, I have found

that in such moments somebody always appears
to save me from myself: great-horned wilderness

armored longhand tank division—I'm just saying
Sometimes it's you in your space ghost slipping, sometimes

a ragged philosophical flight   You try on the argyle
but discard it seconds later   You wonder at heartbeats

by flying a kite   Of course, it's okay if you don't
understand me unraveling this way, because someday you will

(around the bend of your self-same-unraveling-yourself)
and see there a meadow in the dog-eared-before-you

possibilities, ones that you made happen so long ago for me
Uncommonest punk rock beginnings

WATCH ME BLOWTORCH

The wasp pursues its rock'n'roll,
resolutely and unmindful
of the dumb neighbor's dumb
mimetic dog, and for that matter, also,
the maple. Basil plant or chemical, whatever
you want. The wasp dives into the wall
again. Morning waning, and almost noon again,
I'm thinking it's not information
the robins and finches. Meanwhile,
I am at a point on the moon
of a distant planet, afraid
of choking in my sleep
on a dear pile of books: Alphabet,
Physics, and Keats. Or, alternately,
my little daughter beats
on a jumbo roll of toilet paper
like she's the new-jack drummer
for Slayer. The sky wishes everything
otherwise of course.
The words of the day are
radiance and Satan.

MATT HART RUNNING
WITH DAISY, HIS DOG

Running with his dog, Matt Hart sucks in
big hunks of frosted air and then forces them back out
like barely visible tufts of pink cotton candy,

like apple blossoms twisting in the wind, like
shadowy clouds of flying red ants and
a million or so unfinished projects.

He runs as fast as he can (mainly because
he hates to run), then stops to walk and catch,
again, his breath. But Daisy keeps going, going,

gone, until jerking at the end of her adjustable lead,
she turns with a look of sympathetic exasperation
saying, *C'mon c'mon c'mon, let's run fast*

again, grrr! look at that sparrow, that mailbox,
that squirrel, let's stick our head in this pile of leaves,
this one right here, then fling 'em around, fall down

roll over run off with this stick... And so it goes.
It's December and Matt Hart just had another birthday.
36, he thinks, and divides it by three, and doubles it,

and starts running again taking a deep breath;
he wonders, as he often does, about the finish line,
the one which is his own yard, his front door, but also

the one he's seen in his mind, never for long and never
for real, but that one, which, when it occurs to him, stops him
in his tracksuit. Sometimes, he thinks Daisy sees it too.

But unlike him, she runs for it as hard as she can,
There it is there it is there it is, let's go!
But he can't "let's go," can't get over all

the things he doesn't know: How will it feel
to vanish? Will Daisy get a bone?
Will anybody be waiting there to greet them?

LUCID AND BROOKLYN

I wake up in New York, lucid
and Brooklyn. 434 Grand Ave, Apt. 4.,
those people are adorable. I could kiss
their kitchen floor. I could kiss their Brooklyn

Bear. O wrestle the invisible doorman,
Oblivion. Jack-hammered skyway. Appearance
of genius. Two weeks ago I cut my eye
on a cheese grater. It bled a lot a lot.

It's finally healing. Adorable. Sometimes I kiss
its crater. Sometimes even lucid, the moon. Six
weeks ago I ruptured a tendon only running.
Suddenly, I wake up it's Brooklyn. Everyone's

in the room. Even the doorman. Even the skyway.
Everywhere I look someone's famous in Ohio.
Someone's bleeding on the threshold, a lot
or a poem. It's Grand Ave. It's hammered. I wake up

a genius.

LET'S ALL GET DRUNK LAST NIGHT

The best thing about hindsight
is not being stuck in that tree last night.
There were finches, there were clouds
and some other things: pigs' feet,
plastic bags, pants raining down
on the double-shag carpet. And this is where
it gets dirty. Every man, woman, and child
with a shovel. Every lightning bug.
I don't know why every lightning bug,
but I do know last night considerably.
The difference between a bird
and a branch. The difference between
cinnamon and spit. When my face fell out
of its box, I was certain that was it,
but somehow the squirrel doctor
made an impression I can't seem to shake.
If this be voodoo, the more booby-trap
the better. My monkey friend is orange
and you can watch him scatter. Opened
by firemen, I thrive on crooked teeth.
I learned my lesson twice, but now
it's missing from the books. Let us
begin with a landslide of feeling—
a feeling sympathetic for the tree.

GOODNIGHT EVERYBODY

Constellations exhaling,
the moon is full of nobody, the night
blinks its eyes at me and your letter
on the desk. A spoon in my belly,
I needed that—all blown to bits
with a horseshoe. Saddest thing
I ever deserved. I guess I've fallen
pretty down to earth again, off my high
horse or high chair or punk
rocker again. All blown to bits. And now
I can only repeat myself, because
there is almost nothing to narrate.
I go to bed late. I wake up early.
Make coffee. Feed the Daisy. Take her
out. Check my email. Worry wart. Then
when the baby wakes up, I talk to her.
I make her a waffle, plain, and an egg
scrambled. We listen to music. I tell her
I love her. Smiling mostly I have
every reason to be happy, but I am only
a knock-knock joke I won't repeat.
I go to teach. I say some things. I leave some
out. My computer's stupid. Nobody's there
in the rib cage beating. Pretty down to earth
again. I wake up again. I go to bed,
and it's true, man, I don't bow down

to nobody. I have every reason not to.
But now the night blinks like a creature
under water. I tell you and everybody
as always I love you, but I am tired.
I am constellations. Lately I am
second thoughts, can only growl
inside myself. And outside myself
the blowing to bits. So I read the baby
a story, which helps. Goodnight rabbit.
Goodnight old pal. Goodnight kerosene
lamp and glucose and glass of red wine.
Goodnight accordion and boa constrictor.
Goodnight hockey players bloodied in a fight.
Goodnight layers upon layers of signification,
like too warm blankets covering
my face. Goodnight associations.
Goodnight deconstruction. Goodnight
letterhead that made me wake up.
Goodnight clouds, and goodnight
preamble. On to the amble.
Goodnight amble.

MY WIFE ON HER VICODIN KISSING

My wife on her Vicodin kissing. I wish
I had a bike made of leaves. The meat hanging
taut in the house of our dog. I wish
I had a lightning of trees. No lucky cherries

but blossoms all around me, I sleep
in my blowfish, who's twelve stories tall.
The demands of this think tank are naturally
terrific, the deer and the squirrels overwhelming

this Fall. Raining from clouds in the orchard
above me, a tricycle writing itself in my book.
She walks upon water drinking Sauvignon blanc
and takes a few liberties erasing my face.

Who writes writes prescriptions of infinite pieces.
Who hears hears the squeak of our voice
when it calls. My wife on her bike
made of Vicodin kissing. A lightning of trees

tearing through me.

LINES: I AM   NOT JOHN CLARE

I am a barker by profession
I am a badger with a touch
I lean upon the windowsill
    and view the world
        as a pheasant [sic] dream
I wish to be or not
      or else
        always to remember thee
    A mouthful of worms
    The unhinged trees
    Puddocks, buzzards, etc.
I envy them their wings
    I wish the devil luck
    In Allen's madhouse caged and living
    In mellow shades no pencil e'er conveys
    The bookman eats grass, then kicks
      Poesy is over the wall
      Poesy's power, overpowering sweet
I love at long last the breakneck hills
I love to hear the evening crows
I sit on a bench in June ensnared
    and pleased
      in my loneliness
        I long to stay forever
    I snap at the air
      with my solid gold head

Unequalled raptures
Happiest happinesses

HER NAME WAS NAME

I had a girl, I named her soap.
I had a soap, I named her cat.
One day I played the accordion on paper,
and it sounded like a birth certificate
drifting into the sun, a disintegration station
in a vast bewildered wilderness—
which sounds like a slide whistle at first
but later like the back porch flytrap I named
jungle. I have never before mentioned
these names in the airway, and neither has the girl
I named name ever faltered—
though the question of remains
in the hallway remains: Does one's imagination
also disintegrate, or does it flutter forever
like a boa constrictor, circling the world
or a warthog? The warthog I named babe;
the boa constrictor I called pasture.
The last time I found myself ensnared
in the pastoral, I imagined a rope
and escaped by climbing up it.
Then I named it laminate, but I called it
overwhelming. Me and overwhelming
covered in skulls. One superhero
to another to another. I boiled a lobster,
I named it travel. I had an agent,
and I named her mob.

Then I took out the garbage
and went running with my dog
ostensibly to prove my existence,
if not also my purchase. I made a purchase,
I named it purpose. There is nothing so bright
as a toddler on fire. We don't need no water...
I named the water deathstar.

PERSONAL POEM #10

It's 10:14 PM in Westwood it's Halloween
and it's probably 10:14 in Cincinnati
but I'm in Westwood. I'm eating blueberries and listening
to "The Magnificent Seven" by The Clash. The bass line
punctuating my mind like a sentence. And I'm thinking
after reading Berrigan again that Westwood isn't
like Cincinnati without its two or three tiny skyscrapers   it *is*
       Cincinnati
without any big buildings in the sky whatsoever. In fact
I've never been confused about it   not once   have I ever been
more certain than I am now about how to see the sky in Westwood.

                              But I never used to think
I'd end up on the West side at all   with its conservatives and
       Catholic churches
flower shops   chili parlors   and Mercy where Melanie went
       to high school.

                    And I never thought Eric would be
grinding his teeth in his sleep the way my sister did   or be
on medication for anxiety the way I am   but neurochemistry is
a funny sort of burning inside us   perhaps that's all we can say.

                  Regardless   the fact is that
Eric is a genius and so much more courageous than the rest of us
even at things like computer networks and *Teach Yourself*

Postmodernism   which to me just read like an autobiography
I'm not sure whose   and that stung   a little
because unexpected things do that.

                    For example   when the door knocks
it's Mary Anne with her two little boys   Hank and Oscar
ages 4 and 2   coming over to show us their Halloween costumes
(Tigger and Elvis respectively)   and bringing us
more candy because we're running out instead of running over
and our neighbors too   running out   and so have started
emptying their pockets of change.

                            I used to think
by now I'd be rid of Halloween and sadness
        and the happy little faces
of children in costumes   but now I realize   I thought I'd be
a famous rocker like Joe Strummer   who could never die
but did anyway   heart attack   just like that
age 51

HISTORY LESSON

Back before screaming was a new kind of singing
Back before the equinox balanced the durable egg
Back before the back before
    the lemon-ry and Sonia Kharkar's poem called
        Matt Hart's Cat Mao's Personal Poem #11
            as Sung by Sonia Kharkar
Back before the walls crumbled like cookies, and Melanie and I
    would sleep all day, then watch movies in a heap
                        on the floor
Back before the leaks
        the canaries
            the terrific broken toaster that we've had
    (it seems) a hundred years—toast your frozen waffle
      or English muffin on one side, then turn it over
                 and toast it again
Back before dancing and Dean Young,
              space travel and World War I
Back before I skipped a lot of interesting information
    as a means of getting to the point
Back before the brain's damage
Back before my falling-fine with Shauna, my falling-over with
    Christian, my fanatical, my uncle
Back before the vividry
    ((with thanks to Ethan Paquin (for friendship
        and SONNET BOOM, the burning gloom,
        brother, the book) for unwavering FAITH))

Back before REVELATED (a word I think I made up) meaning:

    1) intense spontaneous and illuminated revelry

    2) a state of elated revelation

    3) GALVANIZATION

    4) revolution with a smile

Back before in the day when rappers delighted

Back beyond the back beyond the eight or nine or ten GREAT
    STUDENTS

Back before the death of Dave Otis, my friend of bright lights,
    big city heroin face

Back before the scam in Iraq, behind the barn of huffing glue

Back before the back-brain stimulants, back-brain depressants
    and all night mood swings

Back in black in fashion in style in a sentimental mood

Back before back teeth aching in high pressure systems

Back before invention of the nuclear wheel

Back under the knife for a repeat performance

Back under the knife for a repeat performance

Back before vaudeville, before noumena, before night flights and
    crockpots, before drinking and breaking up at 4AM

Before story problems, before my father rushing headlong into
    eternity's death suit, three buttons down the front and
    a rose in his pocket

Back before I was a liar my soul functioning perfectly

Back before you kissed me on the lips at Ocean Beach

Back before the ocean's beach and Richard Diebenkorn's painting
    of coffee

Back before I wrote this poem and also that song that gets played
    on the radio in Spain

Back before the tribe splintered, thus beginning the never ending
     death of us all
          O killing
               O softly
                    O Roberta O Flack
Back before the black liberationist jumpsuits of Gil Scott-Heron
Back before the first time I told you so, before the lights went
     down at the movie about brain-eating zombies
Before you missed your plane and I missed my arrival
Before the hydraulic soul gave up and gave out and drifted away
     humming beauty beauty O where have you gone?
Before Black Beauty before Over the Rainbow, before I had any
     clue how good Gregory Corso is who said "Man is the
     victory of the world," but also that all of us are "replicas"
Back before I sent the letter to Alex Lemon, saying, care about
     something deeply and then demonstrate those depths.
     It's how we make our experience richer, our world bigger,
     our limits disappear
Back before he wrote back *Mosquito*
Back before I started writing the same poem repeatedly, because I
     keep saying it and saying it but nobody ever hears me or
     they hear me and think I'm an idiot sincerist or for some
     reason I'm kidding I'm not kidding I love everybody I have
     high high expectations and often I'm so disappointed I want
     to stop hurting at the core of the stupid hot earth
Back before idiots ruled the stupid hot earth
Back before the vast and void and VAVOOM! VAVOOM!

Back before the sidecar, the funny car before nitroglycerin
Back before the fruit bat, the treehouse, the ice cream truck,
    the rabbit

Back before it all began and we were comfortable
    and uncomfortable and alive in our shoes, which carry
    us forward to eternity's drool toy, to the moment when
    everything goes blank, or black and white, or sticky and
    sweet
Back before us, a long time ago, there was probably a huge guffaw
    in the firmament, a laughter so violent the sky shook
            and everything started aright,
        but somehow also got off on the wrong foot
                    and some dude in a room
                    pushing buttons or drugs
            said I knew how to handle this yesterday,
                    but Now What?

I COULD'VE SWORN
THERE WAS SOMETHING
I NEEDED TO TELL YOU

but now I only feel my face and neck burning
    in the corrugated tumult of a sunlit afternoon
I'm wearing a t-shirt and jeans, not a suit and tie,
and nobody seems to care that it's greeny late April,
    all of them sleeping through my lecture on Spring

I realize now that the motorcycle cop, up fast behind me
    on my way to work this morning, was a bad omen
After that, even James Schuyler couldn't save the day
"His poems," I said, "are beautiful and shy, full as my eyes
    are full of dogwood blossoms and fog-radio voices

not catalytic converters and omelets for breakfast when simple
    scrambled eggs will do"   "In a dream I loved a girl,
but she exploded," said my friend Scott Dennis, "over
and over   It was all very innocent, but how distraught
    it made me"   I have a feeling, and this is me again

speaking in the present, that I'm failing vividly, or I'm not enough
    innervated, or I'm just not   The gloom inside me hits
the sidewalk, as the shit hits the firmament (and sticks there)
I'm no ostrich   I can take a punch   Mine is only one vision
    of paradise tossed, a kind of asthmatic misery, a kind

of aesthetic grimace-ry   Welcome forbearance to the tree house
        of my disappearance, my delight in substance, my
barrel of walls   When the wallet falls out of my pocket,
I have (I realize suddenly) a million and a half things to lose
        but not one of them is money, not one

of them matters in the eyes of the world—I mean, that is, if
        the world even has eyes, which it doesn't, or if
the world has a clue, which it never will, and by the world, there,
I almost mean God   Dear sir, I have a question, Do I sadden
        myself, or is it You in charge   Among the bad

dreams of exploding true loves and bad omens of lawmen
        and amid reports of another teenager missing
in Florida, another car bomb in Baghdad, these words,
a fragile construction, may in fact collapse on my head
        at any minute   For Christ's sake, somebody
        give us a break   it's Spring

AIR TRAFFIC CONTROL

I'm coming to the end of what I can imagine
life to be: a series of pratfalls, dinners with friends,

men who can't afford even five-dollar dogs. In short,
whatever isn't all bad, isn't much good either, and

the pain is the thing that sticks with me. I guess this life,
like all jars, has its too slick sides, its bottom and lid.

Every morning I wake up late, having spent
the whole night in the mines of my heart, and Melanie

has already been up for hours. Smell of coffee.
Sound of TV. And this morning there's a dead baby bird

on its side in the driveway. Don't say it's just nature;
it's sad. Why? The thing barely even got started,

yet struggled just the same from beginning to end. I saw it
happen. All afternoon yesterday, the mother bird flying

back and forth prodding and feeding it, calling it back
to the tree. *Stupid little bird*, I imagined her singing,

get up and fly like you mean it. No one can help you.
The cats are coming, etc. You are a tiny thing

in the shadow of a giant world. Pick yourself up,
or you will die there... But the bird was sick or hurt

from falling, and that was that. The mother was right—
as mothers mostly are—and the bird died in the night.

So the first thing I do is pick it up off the driveway
with a dustpan—though it's hardly dust—and then

place it under the reddish-pink flowers I don't know
the names of. I don't know the names of birds either.

And I don't say for it a eulogy. I just pitch it gently
under cover of those pretty things, and then

stand there a second thinking, poor little bird. I know
it's sentimental, but helplessness makes me sad,

as do also suffering and the ends of things—both,
it seems to me, relevant here. Thus, I keep returning

to the beginning, which is right where I, and everyone,
started out, but also where we all keep hovering.

I'm not here to say that everything has to make sense.
On the contrary, I'd say most things have not to, so that

the order, or the Absolute, or whatever connects us,
can keep defying our logic, and also our souls

in the heavens/ the darkness—to cajole us into living
the best way we can.

LIGHT-HEADED

(2010)

NOW SHOWING   OF FALLING

Now showing   of falling
Technicolor maple   September Midwest
Who cares more and who cares less   Nobody knows
if I don't   This daily-ness   recorded recording   art or
not art   current events
Leaves of Grass   *Iron Chef America*
I feel cheap, but heavy-duty fine   My friend Dobby
says "giraffe" in a letter   says "tops"
and possibly
"little appropriation"   says "baby" and
                        "the only thing worse than feeling
this way/ is not having a reason to feel this way"—is not
        having a reason to feel   O agreement
floor to ceiling   I'm with you   esp. in light of
the tiny poem I found scrawled in the margins of my alarm
going bonkers   warp speed uh-   head—
my own   eyes awake wide in the red sunlight
Cincinnati's my favorite moment
and's unfolding ever
and sometimes after   Thirteen years and counting
birthday cake candles   front porch azaleas   Melanie
Jackson   Daisy   now Agnes!
Lovely Insulation   vs.   Robot Paranoia
Crumbling driveways   sinister bushes
plank-walking   pool-sharking   neck meat
                    the sky

O flight of meaning
of kite string erupting for the very first time   I mean
a bird's nest not an image   I mean a depth-charge
not a grave   So far so good   so
rockets prove nothing   or almost
hereafter   convince me

CLOUD VS CLOUD

Vast vs. Void

The moment of Truthing.

People telling people through ski masks, Hello.

The anger of swans.

The sadder gallbladder.

The removal of everything harmful from water.

Dogs loving dogs.

A weightlessness question.

A question of patience and what will make good.

The goodness of a promise.

The translucence of a psalm.

Three hawks in a phone booth, two in a stall.

O infinite pieces.

A throat full of wishes.

Gods loving dogs.

The liver/gallbladder.

The removal of stones.

People telling people through a glacier.

The angry Beautician

The goodness of swing sets.

Shark vs. Hearse vs. Wonder

forever.

SERMONS

AND

LECTURES

BOTH

BLANK

AND

RELENTLESS

(2012)

LAMPLIGHTER

It isn't any clearer to say it straight out
The angel and the devil, one body and nobody
To be a better perversion, a person with a mouth
I want you with me   the white-green clouds
and the thousand screamy, on fire recordings
of speaking over the water a shadow in our image
The two of us missing our turn in the sun,
but making our connection in the here-to-ever after
We make the meaning   We blast the giving
insistence terrific   one vision   all of us
more vehement than different, and these words
for what they're worth, cascades and some salvation
Reminders of throwing ourselves against the wall
Myself and yourself and laughing and drinking
to wake us back up after long living hell
Wake us back up after fire-breathing blackout
You ghost, you owl   It isn't enough just to wait
One person's apocalypse, another's brilliant rapture
This message much slower, my call for your response
Don't die on the porch or anywhere else   Life is
our eternal nature   Lamplit reflection
in the prehistoric dark   Sermon bubbled over
in the obvious present   Red tricycle   This beer
with black pepper   For the longest time I thought
the "lying mess" in the lyric was a "lioness" out to get me,
and today it snowed a lot or a fever choked me up

I talked on the phone to my friend about the future
My heart started going   Fits of leaves of Whit-
maniac grass   I tickled my daughter   The house
caught fire   Deeply this winter   Or in summer
all at once   One always has a choice
what to do and what not

from SERMONS AND LECTURES

*

The snow the snow   It fell for two days
It fell   has fallen   Richard Hell and the Voidoids
What's lost in the fix   Nothing and nothing
but notation's notation   Looking out the window
at my life's repetition, I don't begrudge it   I take it
to lunch   Swiss cheese and Triscuits   The clock says
panic, so forget about reading   You listen with your heart
to the flutter of blood   It was cold   I felt Satanic
Two new stories and a dream of Metaphysics, a dream
of the classroom, I forgot all the words   So you went out
to build a man in the powder   Came back freezing in a tangle
of birches, and my legs fell asleep watching over the shepherd
Wake up legs   With love   Yes, please   My friend
driving home and one hundred twenty accidents
People sliding off the road, cars flipped over and trucks
like ballerinas   To say mess would be an understatement's
understatement   White knuckle driving all the way home
Oui Oui Oui   If I had to fill in the Blank Generation
I'd get even more out of breath, then I'd say
whatever you want   I got a hole in my universe—
chorus universe chorus, yeah!   I'm the new noises
and also all the old ones at the very same time
Orange notebook and loving your presence
Look out the window at the birds and the fishes

When we fall we're the Devil, but when we rise
we're redemption   City elm City elm   My couch
to my yard   Azure is a fancy word for America
where once I heard singing, which is just finery with me
I've got more la-la than "medulla oblongata"   Hear it fly
It's on my sleeve   This sermon on snow
and early punk rock   I will not engage in argument
Let the Kierkegaards and Whitmans duke it out
with the critics   The Kierkegaards and Whitmans
will win every time   What I got I got
by sitting still and laughing with my little girl
Hell is always better when it's blasting in the kitchen
And nothing's always something when it's followed
by tonight

*

Tonight tonight   I stay in the room sweeping
There's a lot on the floor, Arborio rice   and beaches
some thousand novel pages   In the mail arrived
a vortex, terrific unexpected   This voice is to distortion
as frost is to a preacher   A class of raging fire
The roof is rather weeping   I'm so thrilled about
my notes on negation and also the ones on a dissonant squall
I can see their faces and their faces are the rapture
I play the eternal with my life paratrooping   Piglet pajamas
and the news I remember   Feb. 2nd 1979   I was at my
grandma's watching TV in the basement, emaciated weirdo,
but the danger felt like music, organs spilled about
on the sidewalk for the crows   The crows that care less
and even less-less the pigeons   David James, the anchor
man, Channel 14 and the ten o'clock blast   More than
thirty years later I'm a typist falling fine   Stupid
Sid Vicious, even dumber Johnny Thunders   Lightning
remains a thing   I love to watch it sprawl   There are moments
when it feels like it's reaching out to touch me
And then you show up with some flowers or pasta
What could be more minimal, befuddling, and true
The idea of people is an idea when it hits me   Wherever
I'm breathing and wherever you roam   And not
just any people, but you know who you're bleeding
You'd better wake the teacher since it's history fleeing
And now we're in the moment we can blow the fucker up

To flood the nomenclature, to further our ambition
and murder the carcass of everybody's winter   Durable reactor,
I wanna be as relentless as you are relentless   No matter
how old or how high in your jaw   There are things
so at random that the monster stays focused   Even looking
stupid, I'm aglow

*

Mote/Emote   I'm not there yet   The electric
connection connects us, nevertheless, at the nexus
between two construction sites, one with cut paper,
one with wooden blocks   After all the cityscapes
and birds melting off   The alphabet survives us
and begins to make its sense   And in spite of all
our efforts to exist in floral prints, the pep
in our steps isn't remotely about Wire   Not
"Field Day for the Sundays"   Not a flag of any
color   Pink covered Agnes from the moment
she was born   From the moment she was born
ever after and before   One deep breath was all
it took   The meadow goes on holiday   The system
goes and goes along   Consuming and growing, but
eventually you die   When are you gone   And when
is it knowing   Never greener, the grass stains
My fingers, my forehead, the knees of my pants
When the word comes over the speaker it's bloody
These instructions I don't get more or less   I get
richer ground to stand on, as the magma breaks
a sweat   I remember once   Something cherry
Japanese   This is my first ever lecture on spring

AMPLIFIER TO DEFENDER

Just back from running—it seems I am always writing you
when I'm just back from running, but that's what happens:
My mind in motion works better in motion, or maybe it only works
more furiously. Or happily, clearly, seriously. My plan is to make a few notes

on who we are/what we might be. What it's like
to pay a particular kind of attention, have faith, get reckless. To unravel
in our pockets and in sadness, fall or drift or tear apart. Last night
I cut my finger on an artichoke. I reached into the refrigerator,

and it was thorny and sharp. Today it hurts. That's not a diversion,
but a reminder to stay focused. Now looking up at the clouds
from my porch, I am thinking how nice it is to be entangled in all the ways
we are—what we think, who we love, and the grand scheme   of things.

There's always a grand scheme of things even if we can't articulate it.
I think one can see it in the fact that anything exists at all. Cities
and locusts. Speed metal and snow. But if one doesn't,
that's okay, too. I'm not really invested in proving some   fleeting thesis.

My assumption is only that we all have assumptions
and these have a great deal to do with our perceptions. The world
as I find it is similar to and different from the world as you find it,
so it becomes necessary for both of us to find the common ground,

the plateaus and sore-spots where our hearts and our language
and our dreams overlap in a bridge that we can walk together.
As Lyn Hejinian notes, "Language, unlike other artistic materials,
doesn't only exist "in multitudes of contexts, it *is* multitudes of contexts"

and given that there are multitudes of languages, you can see
how reality doth spiral out of control. Depending on your perspective
I suppose this could be thrilling or terrifying or both. One can't be
out-of-control-in-control—that is, both reckless and careful all at once—

and yet, in a significant way with words we always are. We employ
and deploy language simultaneously—it is, by its very nature, both
a thing that we use to mean other things and a thing that means out beyond us
in spite of our best efforts to keep the portrait in focus, e.g. "I cut my finger

on an artichoke. I reached into the refrigerator and it was
thorny and sharp." The artichoke or the refrigerator? Both.
And I love that. I don't want to fix the ambiguity. I want meaning
to radiate. I want to make sense, but I also want sense to be made of me

(both by myself and other people) and regardless. As Matthew Rohrer put it,
"I must learn to say the things I never intended to say" and then
I want to add: I also want to learn to say all the things I intended to say—
intended and unintended in the very same breath. This seems to me a power,

inherent in language itself, to make and re-make, to vision and re-vision,
to act and re-act to the world as it throbs, or culture as thesis-antithesis-
synthesis, fear and some trembling necessary and full. Barbaric yawps!
Walking home drunk the other night, I said a bunch of weird, good things

and you did, too, and while it's hard to remember exactly what,
the shadows of what and the feelings still linger—even now,
even sober—we were so fired up, because
the night was so ridiculously in flower, so and so and me and you

electrified and shocking, terrific and true, and we were laughing together,
leaving our strung-out presence like presents around the city,
me an amplifier and you a defender. One thing I definitely remember
is talking earlier—earlier when?—earlier ever

about how you convince everyone that you're talking directly to them,
and I convince everyone I'm dangerous with speed—it's true
I like being worn out, even when I read, and sometimes, too, overwhelmed
and even panicked (though mostly after the fact). When experience kicks me

and everything turns black, or polka-dot, or mechanical bull or post-avant,
my teeth in the trees my blood on the windshield, it's just an indication
that I need to act decisively—to do something for myself with myself
and keep living. It's the best I can do for the people who'd miss me,

but more importantly for the ones who I would miss terribly. Life is overwhelming
for good and for ill. But what isn't overwhelming? Beauty is overwhelming.
Data is overwhelming. Text and the devil and the heavens overwhelming...
How to live and what to do? To make sense all the time (or maybe ever)

in this life/of this life is a sham. Nothing is perfectly nailed to the wall.
I want as much as possible for the carnival of what is. Better worn out
and wary, than a mannequin pretending. "The slightest loss of attention
leads to death" said Frank O'Hara. I say be prepared for the darkness

when it takes you, but stay alive and stay light
for as long as you can.

from BOTH BLANK AND RELENTLESS

*

No performing animal-eagle   The snow
the now   The people come around, stop loafing
in the ether   rhetorical bombs   launching
and lofting metaphorical missiles, distortions
of the facts, which laid out rightly are all and inclusive
Nobody's grip comprehensive, but all of us
living and drinking, loving and wallpaper
fucking the totality as we are its it   Don't wait
for the map of human being   Might as well
wait on the corner for some flowers to appear
from the mouth of a stranger with a briefcase
cutting cocaine against a window or a stranger
with a stranger haircut wearing combat boots
and breathing Anarchy, State and Utopia,
Robert Nozick   Might as well red devil
in the morning and heaven after supper
Today I feel—or rather I felt—something eager,
but then as an afterthought I got up and figured
something out   More similar than different
I want to include you in the electrical circuit,
in the electrical socket, we plug each other into
emergency convulsions, which is getting acquainted,
which is forming a new more inspirited constellation
in the shape of being together reading and writing

our separate, but similar and sexy green books
on how the earth is getting warmer, so we take off
its clothes and our clothes, but nothing seems to help
except weeping in the icebox, but cars get between us
and religions get between us and politicians especially
make a living of between us, of for an' against us,
of weapons and races and beards vs. beardless
and blacks vs. witless racist bastards vs. all of us
we gotta stop making so many damn distinctions
The fabric of America frayed all around the edges,
frayed even in the center   The new Black Panthers
and the dopey white answers and the drill baby drillers,
the foreign investors   All my balls
in the air   It's a wash   Gravity calls
So I'm calling for a blending, not into the scenery,
but into each other toward a common understanding
What ails us *is* us, and what us is is all   We face
each other to answer each other   We begin
by shaking hands or with some other greeting
We sit at the table and we listen

*

Once upon a time before   Happily ever after
I came to dance, but I ended up quitting
At least it seems like that's what happened   What was
and what was happening   A natural disaster
The if-y architecture   The throatless opera singer
and your pelvis on the beach, forty starfish in the sun sort of
breathing and tomorrow always yearning our thesaurus
to extinction   The Dead Boys and The Flesh-Eaters
This autobiographical   Marigold teeth   This maybe
something shriller   Some notes on notation,
a slide presentation   A philosopher's midnight
in a cellar drinking cognac   Darby Crash's suicide
My blood brother/sister   Aphoristic heavy-water,
happy stupid sniffing glue   People nowhere better
than the place they started breathing   Let there be
honey   The body starts its failing with the shadows
falling lightly   Clangy folding metal chairs   The lovely
untold story with its view of something different,
not better or greener, but happier and meaner
I do everything with you   And even when I don't
there's some beer in the fridge
I'm home   Are you home
It's amazing

*

Relentless or reckless   Bubble up to the surface
To end all thought, as the body gets lost   A braying
in the ether   A critical condition   Grapefruit beer
with an owl on the label   Japanese writing   White
crayon on a cloud   forgetters forgetting how
they used to be candy   And screwing our faces
when we couldn't make a difference   Turn up the music
and disappear forever   Lake of fire, crystal meth, heaven is
whenever in the uprooted house   Too much pressure
when the death sentence rattles   I sentence the sentence
to a lifetime of racket   Back and forth blasting this series
of lectures   The animals ferocious as they drive us
to the wall   This is one way we string meaning together—
meaning: together we are better than distracted or apart
The tears and the tears should be emphasized both
When I pick you up later, we'll happily ever after
or we'll wallow in grass stain through the blood
from the get go   My mouth so shattered I can almost
taste the devil   The sea urchin jello   The large or small
engine   Coleridge and Corso   Poly Styrene
and Whitman   I sing the vanished body of electrified moss
A planet of snowmen in every direction, and you
with a litter of new-fangled puppies   Our friends
with their kickstands hanging out to be empty
Complexion or complexity   I'm dazzled by your beauty
I'm tramping in your froth   So much mewling,

but I see no evil, or I see only evil   It all adds up
to harder and faster the robots' collisions, and the factories
of atmosphere and everybody so high that the ceiling
is the new floor, and when it collapses the birds, so frightened
and hollow, look to us for reassurance   Never look down
and the water-wings will hold   Now's the time for X-ray specs
A thousand barrettes and the Fluorescent Condoms   I want
this to be special, and I think the vision's flowing   Or
flowering and floating   The winged things panic
when we tell them not to panic   We hit the ground
hungry, and they fly into a painting   Two or three never make it,
so we snap them with our jaws   happiest happinesses   One by one
we pick them off   Our appetites as massive as a giant white hole
A universe born every second when you scream it   Run,
naysayers   We're the supernatural soul   The music
pouring out of us only wants to make you part of us, part
of an order including disorder, including all the fire, both over
and under, you suck a lot of water, but we're here to make you
actual angels, not tourists   We're here to connect
with that bone in your jaw   It only takes a second, and
you won't know what hit you, won't know whether you're coming
or going, forming or reforming or a sea floor of clouds
Gargoyle delightful   Brief moment of fission   Everybody
clap your hands   Clap your hands

DEBACLE DEBACLE

(2013)

DUDE, GO WEST

The house smells like bacon
and everybody knows it, so I won't bother
with description, other than to say
Saturday. Drunk last night
I missed The Wrens. Tonight I will miss it
as well with my soul, the world
growing orange and the horizon television.
I'm drifting and bored in a half solid state.
I called Brett and said, You're it.
It isn't noon yet, but a thousand degrees.
Culture so blown at the edges it's paper.
I bet the next years will be painful for strays.
Home is where I'll wishful stay
tuned to the feelings that twirl
in the margins. I wish Brett would call back
or Evan or Jane, Russell or Merrill. Agnes
is hiding. When you answer I can't be sure
it's really me, so hang up
and go outside to suck some sky
beneath the city tree. One of my neighbors
is down on her knees, and another
whispers sweetly to his mailbox. I start
to walk around the block, but detour up
Montana and head toward the library.
It's another day of Being. Something
straining on a chain. And before I know it

I'm wailing. I mean crying at the word
ferocious, because everything
overwhelms the wussy spirit's defenses.
Cloud-stain rolling on the afternoon horizon.
I'm wishing enamel, then running to avoid it,
talking at strangers to find my own feet:
conducting a vision that's blurry at best.
I detour over some growling description.
I hang up. I die. It's really me, Brett.
Agnes still hiding. In plain sight
the answer. I count to a thousand.
Montana.

RABBIT RABBIT

The winter the winter. Head full of garbage. First
snowy day. It's Ezra Jack Keats. It's weird
   with my coffee. The little girl's puffy coat,
      lavender, and pine-green wool hat—I don't know

where I'm going, frosty around my temples
      and the whole scene smacks like a wrestling match

   between living and not-living, ghost and not-ghost.
Beyond this world is a world, I'm convinced,
   and that's all I'm saying. Or I'm saying there's
      a world to convince myself what is. My belief

neither clear-cut nor clearly definable. Modus Ponens.
      Constructive dilemma. Aristotle, his skeleton

   notwithstanding my living room freezing, bumbling
around in the new morning light. It isn't logic.
   Logic even limits the birds in flight. Whereas I'm trying
      to get out of my own way, looking out the window

taking notes, hoping maybe it'll send me. My face full of pining—
      my eyes rather doughy—my mind unimaginably

   halogened whitely! But that's not right. Everything
that is is imaginable, and everything that isn't is

an unassuming black forest... Even then. Scrambled eggs.
    The world whistling fortune. The lamb

disappearing in the mouth with its tooth. I'm trying
    here to tell you the first winter morning, and also

    that our words are the fences for swinging and knocking
back and forth the unsayable missing. If you can say it,
    it's one thing, and if you can't, it's probably everything.
    Big mouth makes a star, then begins its undoing.

Stop. Start. Telephone ringing. My head full of metal—
    though at first it was landfill—then football and money.

    The little girl with her fir tree. How to think terrifically.
The winter and pink. The sun out and reckless.
    My first rabbit rabbit, so pink brown and white.
    Going out fighting. The other great Keats. Mouth
    running over, running bright.

WANDER-LOST

Here it is another day, ridiculous and fleet
Another day of ticker tape, birthdays
    and death days   And your poem
    of flying so blue in the blue
while mine's a China unicorn I use to pop
    balloons   Why not make everything
        ecstatic, dramatic, a little bit

fuzzy?   I'm not too nifty, not too stunning
Between one line and the litter box, I need to go
    running   Philip Whalen, Wallace Stevens,
    at the mind and at the mouth   I'm frothing
over music—thank the sky for Adam Fell,
    Johnny Sunshine's melted fadeout   Lately
        I wonder will my luck hold out?

Will yours return brightly as a donkey in an airport,
a suitcase on fire with a thousand nuts and bolts?
    How that might happen is beyond
    any of us, but the puzzle's always
better than an answer to the question (paradox,
    predicament, conundrum, the cold)
        I take these things as given

and the joy of our existence   It's the "coming to
conclusion" that's wildly overrated, THE END   I won't

complain even one single molecule, not carbon
or hydrogen, the atmosphere of Mars—
which is so much more beautiful than the descriptions
    in the brochures   Even you
        can be assured   My cheeks are sort of

red, but that's nothing   And the cherries are ripe,
but that's a lie   When you're hanging upside down
    and your blood hits the ground,
        don't imagine it's slaughter   Imagine
you're a planet, and we all can't wait
    to visit   Bing bang bong!   A fast poem
        takes forever, because it's

nothing but jumps—which get the body moving,
while they take the reader's pulse/the writer's
    throat—if we're lucky   I mention that
    only because it's a question you posed
and I do my best at answers, though
    I mostly come up short   Man O man, O
        astronaut, we travel a lot—you flying,

me driving, or a train in the morning to the next to last
stop   This is some serious gazelle vs. cheetah vs.
    suddenly I'm 40 shit!—a thing on its muzzle
    in a gurgle of starlight—which clearly sounds
pretty awkward (or pretty and awkward
    I'm not sure which)   But look
        where we've come from

and how far we're headed: into the red
    roaring weeds of something different,
      onto and unto a savory-sweet bite
It might be a soundtrack overrun
    with hyenas, or everything happening
      with a sharpness all at once

TO YOU AT 40 FROM ME RIGHT NOW

You are four and I am forty, and it is Friday at 4:40
in September, 2010. I have been waiting

for this moment to tell you some things,
or maybe this moment has been waiting for me.
It's hard to know much of anything, but

everything seems in perfect alignment,
and I am not one to argue with perfection

when I can find it, but I do take issue with the way
things seem. Here is a grain of salt for you
to take me. The two of us kicking a ball in the yard.

This morning we were running late, and when
you couldn't find your rabbit you cried, so I helped you look

for her, but I couldn't find her either. You took a pony
to school to show your friends instead
and I came back to a mountain of work

and looking some more for your rabbit.
Another cup of black coffee. Another list to check off

this weirdo frustrating life, this stressed-out every second,
this incredible constant scribble. At breakfast
you made a drawing for me, and we talked about expression.

I showed you pictures in a Cy Twombly monograph.
You said those are just like "me" and then

one of the sculptures you compared to the bones
in your arm, and I thought of dinosaurs, but didn't
bring it up, and when I showed you the Basquiat drawings,

you pointed to one with a coal black face, "That's me
when I'm angry" and a few pages later

you were tickled by a "monster" with "one pink ear
colored pink." "Why is that one pink," you asked, and I said
because expressive works aren't necessarily about the way

things look, but about the way the artist feels and thinks.
You made another drawing with bright fast strokes.

Rabbit exploding with a runway tongue, devil-blue devil
in a suit with a contract. Everything happens so fast
I can't take it. Yesterday is already tomorrow and the next day.

The grass and the leaves on the trees stay green,
and then suddenly it's Halloween, it's July, I'm in China.

You're in Martha's Vineyard. You're at King's Island.
If you're reading this poem, I am seventy-six, or maybe I am not.
You miss me or I miss you, or we miss each other,

even in the midst of being together. It is always this way
with people. Call me right away when you get this.

THE END OF KUBLA KHAN

It's 6:40 PM on Saturday, and I'm not feeling
like a poem   I type "April," and the computer
tells me the 9th, 2011   I'm tracing
a Ted Berrigan sonnet with my finger—or I was
twenty seconds almost ago—and drinking
the Malbec that Melanie bought just this afternoon
to save me
                    from frustration after frustration,
grading nobody's papers   I get so angry doing
busy work/assessment when I'd rather be reading
An Anthology of New York Poets, edited by Ron
Padgett and David Shapiro, or *The Time
of the Assassins* by Henry Miller, and
it bums me out
                    that I don't think any of my students
really like my poems the way I really like their poems
with all my heart, which is a problem
and also
                    I still haven't started writing
the introduction to the re-issue that Nate's doing
of Paul's first book, *In Baltic Circles*, which is
a terrific book, and if he were here right now—
that is, Paul, not Nate—writing this poem,
I bet he'd interrupt it with an advertisement
or a public service

announcement
You've just won
a trip to Nigeria or that cloud above your house
is This Lime-Tree Bower, My Prison,
and the vocabulary would be so fucking
unbelievable I'd need a dictionary just to get
the wiring, but not to get the music,

because
he had an ear like a bird,
and no, that simile doesn't make sense,
green and yellow wings against a dopey blue sky,
but it's spring, and the ones I saw today were
so surprisingly for real and exactly like that
I wanted to offer to buy them

a drink
Thanks for being birds and coming home
to roost   I guess it's time to face the fact
that Paul Violi died

pancreatic cancer
one week ago tonight
which totally explains why he never answered
those last two emails about the Acks
and his Bio   I sent them on Sunday
and he was already ether, habituated to the Vast
with Samuel Taylor Coleridge

RADIANT ACTION

(2016)

from RADIANT ACTION

★

The spring comes, I get it   Dear blazes,
I get it   Knuckleheaded jumble   All the best
mouths of music   All the slick alarming blur-clocks
So now we're in the yellow cake, but not sure
what to make of it   The radio on as usual,
and I want to tell all of you who will listen
just a few bastardly things, and warn you, too,
about the demons and the monster-headed militias
Now I'm a bluebird three days in a row
I sound like Paul Revere in here, the boy
who cried   Code Orange Kids   But you should
really listen to the angel dust falling   The skinny jeans
of Icarus   Pay attention to the way
the hardcore and noise mix with the ambient
swoosh of pond water   I'm so sick of people my age—
especially when it's me—saying people your age
don't have anything to contribute to a better life
tomorrow   Well I'm here to tell you (whatever
age you are, wherever you're from) most of us are
wrong   I am always wrong   Some of you do
care, but some of you are wilted rocks
The zombie apocalypse is already upon us
People pouring people in the streets like beer
That sounds stupid I know and I fear, but I'm afraid

of almost everything, so now I'm forced to dream it
Looney Tunes plutonium   Field reports explosion
Violence spreading violence even into
the geraniums, the Bradford pears, the fucking
golden apples of antiquity, now a brand new fall of Troy
Militants and nuts keep stockpiling weapons
Politicians beholden, don't act in our interests
I can't do a thing about any of it   What do I know
Mediocrity   Second tier poesy masquerading
as The Bomb   Desire is a lifeline, but not
when we get greedy, not when it covers us
in sores and eruptions   Recently, a friend
observed my thing-to-thing-to-thingness, and wondered
out loud why I don't dig deeper   I don't dig deeper
because my bulldozer's broken, and even if it wasn't
what's a lot more dirt, churned up to cover up
the costumes and the failure   I and you and all of us
It's not very optimistic   I'm sorry   I need new glasses
joyfully   That frost on the horizon isn't Jesus
it's a blade   And when our heads leave our bodies,
they're not on a mission   They're just a box of sleepy
hollows, baby-crazy rabbits   Do you get it,
the interference, the lack of solutions   I can give you a hug
and even really mean it, if that's what you want   my one
and only spark   But now that I'm a dying star
I'm making my last will and testament to swallow
everything in my path with an awful, grainy fleetness
All the guns and all the swans, and all the people praying
Hacking and heaving and coughing up blood   I'll be

the greatest omission, and no one will miss it   People,
poor people, the whole stupid planet   This
grave-on-my-face look's alchemically delicious
Let's all cheer wildly
at the end of this sentence

★

My inhuman being   Adrift in contradiction
Why align oneself with anything limited
One can take a whole great lake in one's mouth
The robin in the nest outside my window
with her eggs   Right now outside
my window with her eggs in the rain

Inside, my books break a sweat
just to whisper ordinary language,
how to do things with words, how to
discover in this cricket-y machine

a spirit well-hidden, a pomegranate seed
We plant it in America and grow it up
and teach it to read the looks on the faces
of children   Constellations   The devils
are in me, the angels are in me   Cat piss couches
and sweet kerosene in me   My mind crushes
everything   I crush a can on everyone   I fall
in love in every dream   In every single poem

I die of exposure and heartbreak and aestheticity,
that quality of art that reminds us we're alive,
that fills us with desire and empathy and light,
the engine of beauty, the roar of the sublime

My ears begin their ringing   I'm at work
to wake up typing   The bells of the church
up the street care to chime   And later,
peppered bacon I will wrap around a scallop
I will get a good sear on it   I will think
about the ocean, the pig in its sty

Anything worth saying can be rendered
as an aphorism, might itself be an aphorism,
just so you know   My phrase of the moment

is radiant action   In love with the sound,
in love with the sound, "the pulse
that beats, the breath that flows,
and we'll scream along,"
the anthem goes,
"until our hearts stop"

★

If you must, you must   Open your mouth
Let the light roll out   Ping-pong with books
Fire Fire Fire   Blinding lake water
Weird sisters, blood brothers   Dumb green hands
Come one come all to the wind-up spirit
The time unfolds with fists that shake,
lips that burst   The light is mine, it rolls along
The love is mine, too—is *also* mine   The Clash records
and the skateboards, the devil beside me, the meadow
beside me   The heavy water alphabet, the neighbor-
hood yea sayers of Cincinnati, all my friends' poems,
and my wife on arrival in the driveway after work, so
bewildered and beautiful, while I sit disheveled
and think about tomorrow, this porch, on this porch
The world skull is mine   The hoped-up, hopped-for future
is mine, the vanishment, the robots   But what's more
I *belong* to all of it   We are all of us inseparable
from creation and destruction, the floodlight
of darkness we emit in this life, moreover
the forces we attract, catch, miss   How do we
position ourselves to be our best   How do we
make all this hell into a heaven   Intractable heaven,
awash in the glare-gorgeous glare of it   O happy
new breath—not blood, not hornets, not venom,
not sonnets   I'm asking the questions, because I want
and need the answers   I wake up screaming

my whole throat to red   Today is the day
I'll attempt to make sense   My dumb green
heart is wide open

★

The rain the rain   An echo from before
Or a thousand pinging voices   Gray but not cruel,
a cavernous chorus   I open the front door, watch it pour
over the awning   This house where we're working
and reading this summer
                                      But yesterday we drove
out of this lake-wooded landscape, an hour or so south
to Muskegon's North Shores, a rather desolate place
of empty lots and strip malls, no doubt hit hard
and left flat after auto collapse and no more
manufacturing made an awful ghost of what once seemed
a promise   We were there for Urgent Care,
the closest one to us we could find open on a Sunday
Agnes has strep-throat again   So often now
we can tell just hearing her talk   No throat culture
necessary—though of course we got one
for documentation purposes—and it was positive immediately
when they looked under the microscope—no need to send
anything to a lab in Grand Rapids   Her fifth case
this year, a tonsillectomy in her future   The doctor
in his seventies with a wandering left eye
Were we some relief from his day or a waste of his time
Probably neither   He seemed tired, but kind   The nurses
seemed tired, and a little put-off to see us
                                      Or maybe
I'm projecting, thinking about the waiting

room, a dog show on TV, the mostly Hispanic
and worn-out-looking patients   We were the only ones
like us in the place   And what are we   Luckier
than most, not as lucky as some others   Agnes
got a Z-pac and some Tylenol with codeine for her cough
to help her sleep   Her tonsils enormous, so she wakes up
crying, fever as high as 103   We couldn't wait to leave
that place, and I feel bad for saying it   We didn't fit
there, that gritty doctor's office, that post-industrial landscape
with its saturated loneliness   It seemed somehow
both above and beneath us

                            As we were leaving,
the doctor asked Agnes if she wanted a lollipop,
and yes, of course, she did   We followed him
down the hall toward the exit, and from behind
the reception desk he produced a red plastic basket
of Dum-Dums   She chose something strawberry
without much deliberation   "Would you like another,"
he asked, "for the road"   "No thank you," she said
in her smallest in awe   And when we got outside,
it was already raining   Agnes fell asleep in the car
almost immediately   We put on Songs: Ohia
out of habit and drove back to the house
without talking

★

Circling and circling   I hope you get
the sense of this, the feeling of being
in the world and also not really in it at all—
standing apart from it, observing its distance
from a distance—its murky green lake water,
a face in a window, just a sad floating bulb,
the wind instead of blood coursing through me
as I call   Circling and circling   Come with me
Come with me
                              O the wind
with its cool, but none of us are cool
We go everywhere we go with astonishment
and longing, then stay up late drinking
or humming the newspaper, listening to the music,
the hardcore bands and crickets, factories on the moon
"All our bruised bodies..."
                              The hills
with their trees know everything worth knowing,
calm and clustered, a herd of green lowing,
a pride of green lions   We might surround
the whole place with our love, as fiercely as possible
with an attitude of presence   This place in the sun
This place we come back to   Fuzzy black caterpillar
Enormous black hole   That insect like a tank
with orange road flare antennae

Stillness and children,
a sweet contradiction   Color's abundance in nature
points to soul   Cherries and asparagus
And now we are approaching a moment of resonance
Let the blind spots be sore spots   Let the pang
give us hope, crashing and flowing, so
drunken and perfect   We start at the end,
so the end is beginning   We start
with our eyes wide open   Let's go

★

The difference between noise
and meaningful noise   The difference
between noise and what's meaningful
            And the flat sameness of all of it,
generation to generation, disruption to eruption
I pay better attention when I'm distracted
from the thesis, than when I'm distracted
from expression   I have to work harder
                        This life on the road
This ear to an audience   The duct work,
the basement, the furnace, the stairs
            I wonder if you've ever stared
at a geranium petal and seen all the pain
leaking into the world
                        It doesn't make any sense
at first or maybe ever   But blood is
            being spilled
People are alone
Some of them are even happy about it,
                        but some of them
are lost and wanting something   Some of them
                    are giving   Some of them
have been taken from their homes
            Whole families   Lost tree limbs
    when the wind sets its jaw   I worry
that my worry is too decorative,

that the blue-green wallpaper is itself
the only wall, that hands clasped together,
and that the deference shown, is only for show
   How many times have I wrecked my only
day off in a week in the image of the anger
 and sadness all around it, the silence
between me and myself and my other,
my mother, my father my sister my brother,
the awkward stubbornness, the half-baked
plans to make it better
        Last night
I paddled a boat around a lake—which isn't true,
but sounds more romantic than what really took place—
and looked at all the houses in a circle around it,
the lemon-yellow ones, the moss-blue-green ones,
even pink ones, and one with big red hearts in relief
on its gutters
       I don't know why
the looking matters, or why I liked seeing them,
but I did
        Some of them
are huge places, and some of them are barely shacks
One was recently in a fire From the look of it
I imagine it'll have to be torn down,
all smoke-black and gutted
      But does the lie that I told,
and then admitted to telling, about *paddling*
the boat around the lake, make a difference
I was actually in a boat, but the boat had an engine

Going 'round in a circle with my family
several miles
                It's a prettier circle
without the engine, don't you think
A lonelier circle and more idyllic
without the family

★

I used to think the world was broken

Now I know the world is broken

I sit on the dock of Hess lake and record it
It's gorgeous, meaning all of it
Every little spike of light, the inch
worm in the bughouse   Loneliness

won't be the death of anybody I love
I can promise you that   or anyway, I can try to

Find me as always in Ohio or Michigan, Kentucky
or Indiana, or anywhere else people are all
by themselves of themselves
hard-headed, driven, self-sufficient

Maybe it's only a footnote, but 5.8 miles
is the circumference of Hess
We've been here two weeks and will be here
again   It really isn't far when you run it

Not bad in the water where I try to catch
the ball, the lottery ticket, the strange
stray dog   I don't know about that dog,
or the lottery, but the world is broken,

and some people are broken, even people
I care about deeply   When I tell you

you're lovely, it's a thing you can count on
to be truer every day for the rest of your life
and then some   I don't want it to be
awkward, but I guess it's sort of awkward,
sentimental and flawed after all   Well,

I used to think the world   Now I think
about people   I think about you   I think
about the children   I think about this lake
I keep running in a circle   Nothing in nature
needs fixing

★

All my friends back East   All my friends
out West   And me in the middle of something
sprawling forever   Great blue lake and the sound
of jack hammers, the silence of stars and wind-
turbined horizon lines, a surging resurgence of wavelap
and head-spinning   Pinwheels, sunflowers,
helicopter flyovers   I watch the sun dipping its
face in the water   Pink-yellow-white, a transitional
color   And you walking under the grass in my dream,
another radiant action, another source among sources
Eleusinian   The mysteries deepen   Only puzzles
get solved   Little red-beaked birds with yellow
tipped wings, finches I suppose, but I could
always be wrong   It's even probable
I'm wrong   What do I know about birds
or the responsibilities of co-pilots, of ghosts or the law
of conservation of energy, of vicious or generous
or mossy human being   All my friends   Hairs
piled on the tops of their heads to resemble
every hardcore show I've ever attended in a basement
in chorus, every book I've ever read about giving oneself over
to the absurdity of belief, especially when it's contrary
to all observable evidence and testable hypotheses,
especially in the midst of these lives we bleed, magnetic and pulsing,
our minds and our bodies, such marvelous machines, leaping
with mercy and sufferance and medicine, clutter and all

the impossibly imagined weird worlds spread out beneath us
O accidie of waiting, of writing for something unsaid
and unsayable, unknown and unknowable   The end looms large
at dawn and at dusk   The little girl plays with a dying green
balloon, talks to herself, and when I smile at her, she stops, says,
"What   I'm just talking to myself"   And she's totally right on
We're all talking to ourselves, and our talking makes the difference,
but it's what we say and how we say it, the words we use
and the atmosphere they're carried in   The creation
or destruction we're carried away in   Love and breath
and a thousand glowing muses   It starts as a blues
then builds to a scream, harmonious the dissonance
that we couldn't if we tried to   Then immersion
in the trying in the throbbing this second, the backdrop
of secrets, a before and an after, a silence then a noise
in the airiness all over us, and everything's decidedly different
Sorry somehow

        Still flying radically

        Still falling mightily

★

My veins with your veins, my noise with your noise
If I tell you a secret, will you keep it   Will you
pocket this minute and promise not to spill it   Nothing
subtle about it   Nothing refined   What are we supposed to be

Flour, sugar, salt—some other useful but non-lethal staple
My International Bitterness Unit is high tonight
In the clouds, the clouds, like "the snow the snow"
in those previous poems   Anyone who's ever seen me read

poems in public knows I don't shout all my work—sometimes
we can hear a pin drop   And form and structure
are always a concern   I try and follow the poem
somewhere, let it slide into itself, like a runner

into third   Like a romantic into blank verse   I want
to go home, but I'm not sure where home is   That I keep
failing to get there in poem after poem, book after book,
might mean I'm doing something wrong, or it might mean

what I'm after's in Dante or Coleridge or Whitman
already, so doing something right has to be in defiance
of all my preconceived notions of what a poem's
supposed to be on the page, in the air, in the history

of gravity and clarity and   Fuck clarity   I can talk

the public talk   I don't wanna go home   I wanna go
to Heaven   I wanna get high into—not on—the sounds
of waves, the sounds of words, the poetical riddle   Go ahead

Be enlightened in all the fake, cheap, and standard ways
if you want to   It makes no difference   To be enlightened
is still to be surrounded by darkness   I want to be a light
obliterating everything, the radiance of a thousand suns

all burst at once, but of life not death, with mercy
and splendor   And I want you with me, dispelling
all bewitchment, the shadows cast, and the cast
of shadows   Radiant the action, which is art

and also life   Imagination in defiance of our limits
makes the world

★

My spirit far reaching in the purple far reaches

There are times, like now, when it's fading, I can feel it

But my friend wants to know how I bring it all around,
how I bring it all together, make it coherent,
ground the billion fragments on the fat
of this planet   I am a cow in the mud's his implication,

but I would like to be a bird, as all of this shows,

weightless with worm-wooded feeling,
beyond good and evil, both greenish and close

And outside, my daughter laughs unselfconsciously,
the exhaustion in her voice spilling
onto the porch steps   She plays until she passes

out—every single day   Even the white-sheeted rain
doesn't stop her   Nightfall doesn't stop her
Hunger doesn't stop her   As with all too willful things,

hers is a force of reckoning, a source of abandon—
we should listen, and abandon the world, especially this one,

for all the new noises and some small number of old ones

★

Electrical charge in the current's current current
I can't remember anything that happened
last night after I ordered that fifth IPA, or
from before I was six   It's sort of as if I didn't exist

But I exist   I am being   late afternoon, turning evening
I hear paint cans bleating like shepherds in garages,
eyes of wolves in the darkening light   I don't recognize

my own face when I look   sometimes   and see there
so many trains beating down the tracks of clouds
and other tired images, their heads in their hands, but
their throats full of heart   birthday cake singers

and sutra bringers, down and out wizards and aspiring
punk rockers   I don't want to be alone tonight   But
I am so completely alone tonight   trying to answer

the wide wide gaps in the noise and the music,
the music and the message   So much needs reading into
to sound out in-the-world-in   I go to take a nap in
I go to the window in   Another twilight of six-pack,

another carton of limbo   My feelings
about all of this are both seriously mystical and entirely un-
complicated   I can't begin to get human enough

to do the kind of good I want, so instead I just stand here,
stunned and rocked, my arms around the world
with invisible love   And out beyond this little house,
hungover with spring, the magnolia and its blossoms

are concerned   not   They shimmer in a deep
and treacherous pink   It's too dark to see them,
but I know they're always on, generating power

O radiant, unexpected

Dear Reader

★

"Back in Black"   in the air   at my desk   A mourning
dove cooing an emergency for someone   The plants
in their pots in the white-washed light won't stop
swaying, blow up into meaning—meaning

everything today is full of present intensity,
simultaneity   Guillaume Apollinaire and his dear

pretty redhead   But I'm thinking about what it means
when I drink a glass of water and call Russell or Jen,
Amanda or Nate just to check in and ask them
what they're looking at right now, how it strikes them

in the heart or the head, maybe even the mouth,
and also to tell them today I ran around beheaded
with feathers   In my office I made flyers with Sam
for Adam's reading   I looked at pictures
that Billy took of *Moby Dick* in an aquarium—

not the whale in an aquarium, but the book
about the whale in an aquarium   I just can't
get away from it, this life in the air

all around me, this desk   *Philosophical Investigations*
The sonnet   Even this Touché Amoré t-shirt
that's sweating with activity, more and more
blotto, of beautiful calamity   All the particulars
I have to keep listing, so they won't want to leave me

Lime-green stapler and a yard full of weeds,
the old dogwood tree—at the moment in white blossom,
and all done up with bees for the honey to come   The vatic
Sublime and a puddle of blood   Huge glowing eyes,
wild, exaggerated hair, which is no one I know, but
a painting of John Clare on a postcard beside me

The sound of someone typing   Does it look like your life
when I open my life

RADIANT COMPANION

(2016)

POEM WITH A CHORUS
BY JAWBREAKER

for Sydney Rains

The word is pain,
and the world is pain,
but the sun on our skin
is enormous and light.

I went out running
this morning, the way
I always do, awkwardly

with lightning. And
at some point I thought
about the song
"Chesterfield King"

by Jawbreaker, which is
a punk rock conversation
poem in the romantic

tradition, if ever one existed
after Coleridge and Wordsworth
made it a thing, then abandoned it.
The chorus goes,

"I took my car and drove it
down the hill by your house—
I drove so fast. The wind

it couldn't cool me down,
so I turned it around
and came back up.
You were waiting

on your steps, steam
showing off your breath
and water in your eyes.

We pulled each other into one,
parkas clinging on the lawn
and kissed right there."
The stanza breaks are mine.

I don't know why
I thought about that
then, or why I'm thinking

about it now, except that
it's a song you should know
if you don't already, and it has
a fragility to it, a vulnerability in its lion-

flaming, punk rock heart that
reminds me of your poems, and how
longing never leaves us as long as

we live, which is lucky.
And what's more, I'm suddenly
struck by the image of a rowboat
on the sunset horizon

with one lonely figure
rowing into the distance
out to sea. And in this

image, which is really
the world, I'd like to call out
to the figure in the boat,
to the him or the her,

who is probably you or me or
someone just like us, someone
in need, but they're too far away

to hear me, or I'm too far away
to hear me, and yet,
that doesn't mean I shouldn't
scream and scream

to try and get their attention,
because attention connects us
and generates possibilities, and

possibilities are the stitches
that we use to close
the wounds—the ones
that we inflict, and

the ones inflicted on us.
Yeah, the world is pain,
but attention is rich

and connection changes
everything when we allow it
to sing us, the sun
going down so light

and enormous, the pink
and orange waves,
their marvelous chorus.

I took my car and drove it
down the hill by your house—
I drove so fast. You took
your boat and rowed it out

both to listen and mend.
I'm standing here hoping
to get your attention.

Longing for its own sake
is a letter close to heaven.
Longing and words
continue the world.

REACHING THE AWE SOUND

And I'll try to live defeated / Come and see
The Good in everything / Outside animals sound
Come and see / Then lead us all to heaven

                —Protomartyr, "Come and See"

Here and now, this blue winter sky,
                and outside a light
                      frost,
the windows of the houses
           and the windows of the cars
I walk out on the porch, and my glasses
                  fog up
I start my engine to make things warm
Voices swirl around, as a white-muzzled dog
trots by in this marvel of everything good
                  morning
Back inside with the radio on, the word
in the air is terrorist suspects, videos
of child soldiers executing spies   I wrestle
           the juice from an orange
              in my mouth
I read the beginning of "Song of Myself"
The price of petroleum, a coming election,
a stepped on spear of dead winter grass
              I do not loafe   I lean
on the counter and call for my daughter
She puts her small self in a puffy blue coat

I put my small self in a black wool sweater
                    I drive her to school
                              with the radio off
She spells words with the "awe" sound
          in them,
                    "awesome,"
                              "outlaw,"
                                   "walrus,"
                                        "autumn,"
divides by 9's from 108   At the drop off spot
she gets out of the car   "I love you," I say,
                    "I'll be back to pick you up"
And when she shuts the door, I turn the radio on
Then I turn it back off   At home Greek yogurt
                    with pistachios and pecans   a little honey
                    I drink life down
                              to a hot cup of coffee
This soft daily-ness, my ordinary "yawp"
                                   and "drawer"
                                   and "author"
                                   and "oft"
This picture of heaven, where there isn't any heaven
          is as good a place as any
                    to begin to make a heaven
          "Either we give ourselves to a course of action,
or we do not give ourselves," wrote
                    William Carlos Williams
The rest of the day, I'm mostly messed up
I go "on my nerve"   "I celebrate myself"

I burn through the world with my hands held out

                               Heaven with the radio off

BREAKING SPRING

seems like a good way to say
I spent all last week feeling helpless
and talking about it in terms of not being

Why can't compassion change our lives
even half so completely as a suicide bomber,
or half so immediately as a natural disaster

Big ideas get me nowhere, so
the fact that breaking spring feels better
than cracking up is at least a start

toward a walk through Washington Park,
its trees in pink blossom, its white-yellow-purple
Tomorrow I will talk about *Frankenstein*

in bed and then I will talk about it with people
who are sleeping   I will say that it's a book
about artistic responsibility   I will

say it's alive   It's alive   And some number
of eyes will stare back at me without believing
any of it matters, or without believing

it matters for them   And what can I say
to convince them   I have only my love
to recommend it beyond what it already is

My suspect credibility upon the rockets
of birds, the soft parts of people, the oceans'
inevitable, cyclical weeping   Who has time
for poetry has more time than they deserve

LAST-POEM, TEXAS

Dozing this afternoon, as I have
the last several. The light blasts in
through the blinds, though they're closed.
The train comes by every half hour or so,
blaring its whistle to let everyone know. And Sarge,
the English Mastiff, one hundred eighty pounds,
sleeps in the hallway outside my room,
snoring bravely, the only sound in the house.
I wonder, could this be the last poem
in which he appears? I nod and stir, then nod
again. And the images well-up in a long flooded line,
a ridiculous parade that I forget almost
immediately, but for flashes, like in Coleridge,
only not as strange as Coleridge. All of them
explicable—explicable to me: Daisies exploding
from the mouth of my wife. Menacing shadows
with impossible questions—who knows knowing,
knows what? The Sex Pistols final concert
at Winterland where I wasn't. The chorus
to "Doctor Love" by Kiss, which Gene Simmons,
allegedly wrote in a Holiday Inn in Evansville, Indiana
in the seventies, when I was a child in Evansville,
Indiana in the seventies. What a strange little kid.
I think I was mostly afraid from all the screaming.
I had nightmares and cared about
other people's feelings. I wanted to be

the peacemaker until I was a teenager,
then I was angry for a chunk of my life.
Now that I have my own family, there is
no screaming in the house. I'd say we're all pretty
happy. We're lightning and light. Melanie, Agnes, Daisy
and me. But I've been away some months for work.
Soon I'll go back, and it'll take some adjusting.
The dissonance of seeing and living with ghosts.
Outside now, someone's dumping recycling
into a bin, the waterfall crash of glass against plastic.
I'm completely awake. I'm the calm
against panic, the panic against calm.
And so too the Mastiff, chewing his fake bone.
I can hear his teeth scraping against it
with pleasure. I love and hate
dreaming. It reminds me of home.

IMMEDIATE NEIGHBORS

for Sam McCormick

At a final cruising altitude of 36,000 feet,
I'm thinking about the Chapter called "The Pipe"
in *Moby-Dick* and also about my student, Sam,
who memorized it in her fingers by typing it
one hundred and thirty-six times, once for each
of the chapters in the book, plus the epilogue,
and then performed it for the class, swaying
back and forth, ghost-typing the air to remember
the words, so that Ahab's human struggle became her own
human struggle, and all of us in tears as we stood
there with our wonder. Tough and shocking, a fragile
new meaning. But what triggered this memory, I don't know—
flying maybe
                    in the air next to clouds,
or this young woman, about the same age as Sam, sitting
beside me, and who's coincidentally also named
Samantha, but goes by Sammy, not Sam, she tells me.
She's never seen clouds this close before, having never flown
in an airplane before, so she's taking pictures and can't stop
chattering, popping bubble gum, shuffling her notes for
     chemistry—
she's a chemistry major in Minnesota she tells me,
among other things—and through it all, barely listening
I'm remembering remembering and also some
forgetting.

I can't remember
my first time flying, but right now I'm flying, so that's something.
If I could only be sweeter and meaner, more voluminous,
it occurs to me—I could rise and then fall and then rise—
like Ziggy Stardust and the Spiders from Mars—and then,
if I could write down some chemical equations, maybe take
a few of you with me to Paradise found or Negative Capability,
I would love that to pieces the way I love any linguistic
    associations—
connotation to constellation in a few leaps and bounds.
The problem of the poem is to experience its ending, having
already known so beautifully its beginning, by which I mean
an agony of life and deathery, of music and speech, which is
    given
for a minute, then taken away. The pipe thrown overboard
and lost at sea. Sam's air-typewriter, her struggle to remember.
And this other Samantha, Sammy, she reminds me, her carrot
juice hair and serious green eyes, taking pictures of a plane
from the window of a plane.

          The last three days
in New Orleans I've been a version of sparrows and radio-
activity, and now on my way home to Cincinnati, the Samantha
beside me radiates light, so radiates being. "People only call me
Sammy when I'm drunk" my student Sam once said to me,
drunk, then nearly got arrested driving home
to write a poem.

          And suddenly I'm vividly aware
of all the secrets sitting near me, rising and falling, maybe
rising against me, and I wanna know every one of them.

And also, I wonder if Sam will be okay with this poem? I mean,
the part about her nearly getting arrested's not really my story
to tell—or is it? She was drunk. I called her Sammy.
It all could've ended horribly, but great fortune that it didn't.
Who's story is it? What difference does it make as long as
no one gets hurt? Sam's totally brilliant and deserves
the world's attention, the world's massive love
wherever she can get it, but she's had a rough time
by anybody's measure. Dear Sam, You have beaten
the odds, so you are winning. Be happy. Don't throw
yourself in the drink of any ocean. Keep swaying
in the breeze, ghost-typing
your songs
                    As for the title "Immediate Neighbors," well,
I stole it while sneaking a look at Sammy's Quantum
    Chemistry
notes. Something having to do with particles and the sharing
of electrons, but what do I know? I just read giant books
and lift off. Chemistry's a total mystery to me. The mystery
in chemistry. Coffee, beer, and Ibuprofen. I steal everything
the best way I can, I suppose, from all my friends
and neighbors, the immediate ones and some distant
planets. And with that, we've begun our initial descent.
                    Current weather in Cincinnati is clear skies,
with gusty winds out of the northwest at 10 mph. We should be
getting to the gate just a little ahead of schedule and on the ground
in about fifteen minutes. On behalf of both myself
and the Samanthas, thanks for flying with us.
Flight attendants, prepare the cabin.

ODE TO A NIGHTINGALE

for Russell Dillon

This morning, a sea of summer-
    green in the sky   I'm up early
to go running five miles
    and think about flight for an essay
        Poetry's for the Birds

But first, I do last night's dishes,
    eat a Granny Smith apple, and listen again
        to a voicemail from my friend

Russell, while stretching my blasted
    forty-six-year-old self, which hurts
from playing dodge ball on the trampoline
    with Agnes   Agnes is nine now,
        and her trouncing me at dodge ball

is an entirely different story (so here I won't
    go into it), but in the voicemail, which is
        part of this one, Russell reads

a quiet poem, leaking Freon and sadness, his voice
    a rough blanket   The time signature on the call

says 5:30 a.m., which means it was 2:30
    in California, the state from where he was
        calling, and when my alarm went off

it was two hours after that   The birds already
    chirping their muted green sun   I made a cup
        of black coffee   The dog ate

a soap bubble   The flowers all alight with bees
    softly buzzed   If this seems merely
notational, it is and it is not—"like a daisy in a centrifuge,"
    Russell's soaring poem notes   Sometimes it's necessary
        to record a breaking heart, to locate one's self

in a faraway haunt   Here in Ohio, I put on my Asics
    I run myself crazy   Hüsker Dü in my earbuds
        and an eight-minute mile, then the sound of wind

chimes and "Repentless" by Slayer   Obliterated
    wind chimes   Obliterated clouds
When I get home, I'll listen again to Russell's poem
    I'll write him this poem
        "Do I wake or sleep"

BLUE JAY SLAYER

(2017)

BLUE JAY SLAYER

My wife awake or asleep.
My daughter asleep or on fire.
My brain in the weeds.
Alarmed or alarming.
Disarmed or in panic.
Is it not "doing better" for me to dream
in the eaves? Is it "much worse"?
The earth so badly scorched
that nothing needs mowing, not even
my hair which is glowing with black-
berries, a halo of knobby dark energy.
The phone keeps ringing, but it's someone
Unknown. It's a guy with a grudge
in his pocket, a revolving door
under his tongue. He wants my family
to take shelter in an interior room
with no windows and stay there
until it's safe to appear again in public;
he will tell them when. My wife
and young daughter go missing
in the interim. I go
to the movies. In my bed
I'm watching football. In my lungs
the bloods win it. Then an awful perfection
or a ratchety sound in the leafscape
knocks over us. The air weeps its savings.

I go to the hole. I go
to the sharkery. The train clears
its throat, and I wonder
who's conducting?
My daughter hungover.
My wife a spitting image.
In all the grainy news footage,
the Muslim protesters look bored,
or they look happy to be a riot,
since usually there is nothing else
to do in the village. Smoke billows out
of an Exxon or a mosque. I listen
to Slayer, but the blue jays in the tree
that I am falling toward are louder.
The grackles are louder.
I have been louder, but today
I am yearning. I tell the birds
I miss my family, and the blue sky
falls to its knees in mock grief—
little blue feathers
from my pillow in my teeth.

HOW TO DO THINGS WITH WORDS

The sound of the train and the breeze
take me whistling. I walk a strange street
where a greenish light floods the world,
but only for a second. I am wrestling

with how green isn't really green here
in this not-at-home state, and wondering
if green is ever really green anywhere?

And could this line of thinking, by virtue
of its subject, be pastoral? I doubt it.
I doubt a lot. I am having a hard time lately
seeing how to do things with words.

I'm coming down with a cold, and it's clear
it's going to rain, which is odd. Odd that I can feel it
before it happens. And I am still adjusting

to these ordinary thoughts about an ordinary day turning
toward evening, ordinary language in ordinary usage.
But in my head the voice always wonders
if I could've done it better? All this revision

and little revelation. Something about heaven
at the earth's sorry edges. And
something else too about language, its limits.

I will end this walk soon, or I will get
distracted and forget it. I will move on
to a hundred more pressing rearrangements. And back
in my room, the rain will ping the roof of the house

more or less. Just as I predicted. The train always brings it.
I will look out the window at the dark, wet leaves,
the grass-green house that isn't really green,

and the streetlights reflecting on themselves
in punctured puddles. The streetlights don't wonder
how to do things with words. They shine a light,
and it's simple.

EVERYTHING BREAKING/ FOR GOOD

(2019)

IN LOVE WITH THE SOUND

It starts with jackhammers
And the good vibrations
are everywhere, though there's not a beach
for a million years, nor any place near
in the fog of here   Been up all night
worrying under haze of beer
and a tender slice of rabbit, a slice
of its stupid and buttery little heart
I ate it up anyway without even a thought
Plainly, I am blown apart   I miss you, too
I miss you a lot—a leap, I realize, leftover
from the rabbit   But now that you're with me
I hear myself telling you that there are people
among us, who feel the need to dismantle
any sweetness, to tear the loving faces
of angels to pieces   Of other people,
they know nothing   They know
only their own reflections mingled
in the mangled inner circle of the party,
and they know exactly their relationship
to every other body in the room   They have
a cocktail in their paws, and it's the newest
greenest one   They present
a revision of oranges and little fishes
or they present a series of arguments
They are at the center   They are

so refrigerator   They are Scylla
and Charybdis   They are taking us
to school   I do not like school
And when they open their vaults,
when they take off their clothes,
the self-consciousness dribbles
out onto the floor with their shoes
I have been in that position too
Yes, it's embarrassing   But I am
in fact embarrassing   Better to be
embarrassing than never to feel
a single thing—   And you are still
intractable with all your righteous love
Let the hating haters fall to their knees
It ends with jackhammers and lions

WAVES OF GRAIN

Here we come! Pies in the window!
Corn on the cob! Immigrants! New parents!
Foreclosed homes! Down the stairs a lot
we fall! Twisting the way we do business
in the leaves! We are at the office! We are
on the job! So much jumping, la la la!
Tomato plants climbing the invisible fences!
We look out over the vast expanses! We look
in all our pockets! We balance our checkbooks!
American English, this is the time Now! We come
to you with volume! We come with our shirts off,
pedal to the metal! Cherry blind! Cheery blonde!
Jet fruit! The acres! Let us hold hands! Let us eat
the cool linoleum! It hurts the next morning!
We are always hungover! What a summer!
Engine saliva! Toilet melt! Floods in North Dakota!
Fires in Arizona! What a winter! What an autumn!
It's hard to yelp and not sound pathetic! Difficult beauty!
Spring in the cough syrup! Merrily we roll
our giant trucks into a ball! Leaning and loafing!
Barbaric electric! We are not making light,
and not bearing it either! The silos and igloos!
Our luggage all stowed! Our ringers turned off! Look
at the sky, its display of drunken starlets! Look
at the tavern, its kissable drones! Push-up bras
for everyone! Everyday a house arrest!

All our lives another stroke! Hatchet breath!
Money cake! Grab your rakes! Your ones
and your zeroes! Mission accomplished!
Your tongues on a sandwich! The tattoos!
The piercings! Text your favorite blood type
to all of the above! Roll up your sleeves!
The incredible gay rapture! Join us!
Happy hour! Mon. – Thurs. 4 - 6:30.

WHY I AM NOT A PANTHER

Somewhere it's a Friday,
and in Vermont
it is always beautiful weather
whether anybody notices or not.
People are clapping
their little hands at a lecture
both before it begins and later
also after. They are squirrels
in the distance. I am not a panther
because I don't have a tale
to tell you or anyone
about the jungle, but
if I did, I would drink and pass out
on the lawn. We would drink
and pass out on the lawn.
The days would go by
and the days would go on
with a greenness.
I would tell you just how
scary things really are.
But right now I am a creature
of unnameable distance,
the goats singing songs
of interminable swans.
I go home to a wonderful place
but it's only with a phone call.

The people I talk to, the best
in my life. One of them tells me
she is having so much fun
watching a man making a crepe.
"I am watching a man making a crepe,"
she reports, and hearing this I am sure
of the fun on her face.
"Is that interesting?" I ask,
but she is already drifting
and hangs up without me.
Have a drink, I think. Okay.
I drink. We drink.
It is still Friday.
Vermont is still Vermont,
and whether anyone notices
or not, I am not a panther.
I am a father
missing everything.

JOHNNY CASH JOE STRUMMER

Hello, I'm Johnny Cash.
I have just stepped out of a limo.
You should thank me and believe me
because I have written
some really classic American songs.
I myself am a classic American. Sometimes
I ride my bike places and throw F-bombs around
where people can hear them. It's a kind of terror
of the mouth. Mothers cover the ears of their children,
walk away quickly in the other direction.
I am also Joe Strummer. I am not
a classic American, but you can read
all about me and listen to my band The Clash.
I smoke a lot of weed. I drink a lot of Guinness.
I am a dead man, like Johnny Cash.
But I am alive like him as well
And also like him, I have written a lot
of classic songs. "Daddy was a bankrobber,"
I used to sing. I have been planning this
reemergence for ages, but I have been here
all along. Yesterday I was standing
in my front yard with a garden hose
watering the petunias and lilacs
and all manner of geraniums, and people were
confused, wondering how I can be
Johnny Cash and Joe Strummer

and why I'm a dead-alive man
and all that. Well I'll tell you.
First, I'm a fucking classic, like I said,
and classics never die. They're always
alive even out beyond the bodies
strewn in the streets
of all our cities. I see so many bodies
on the streets of our cities, sleeping
in doorways, rolling around
in drainage ditches, pushing
stolen merchandise in stolen shopping carts.
Everywhere I look there's a newspaper
president. Some of them ask me
for change, but I say change is inevitable
or I sing about "a ring of fire"
and everybody calms down and goes
about their business. Second
when I did that duet of Bob Marley's
"Redemption Song," I thought,
this sounds pretty good.
I should make us forever,
so that's what I've done.
And when I talk to the cats
in the alleys or the chickens
in the darkness, they always ask me
to sign their fur and their feathers,
and of course I oblige. I sign them
"Best wishes always,
Johnny Cash Joe Strummer."

And if I ever do disappear
you should really be worried,
because that'll mean something's gone
horribly awry. Something's skipped out
of the deep groove of the planet
and you'd better probably check
the classified ads and the help wanted
posters and the wanted posters
because the Sun's gone out
and Four Horsemen are stirring
the apocalypse.

BLASTED IN THE SOFT
AZURE MOUNTAINS

Blasted in the soft azure mountains
of Beer, I walked to the ship shape
on the horizon where I found
a Mayflower blue replica of a pilgrim.
In its pocket was a key to the garage
door I'd been trying to open
since the fountain mist had rusted
the lock and knocked me back
against myself where I found you
this Pacific pearl

THE POWER IS WRONG

Cherry pits and stems on the edge
of the kitchen sink. I'm already
baffled how this didn't go my way.
I thought I might write the phrase
"cherry red jeep," because you
told me I should, but instead
I've wound up on the threshold
of some imaginary idyll eating cherries
and looking out the window
at my neighbor not watering his tomatoes.
Dot dot dot. And that I've already spent
three weeks in this state says something
about how reluctant I am to brag
about it, but nothing about why
opening my mouth hurts so much.
Maybe it's the roasted Scotch Bonnets
I downed in a shot, eyes welling up
in the heat, because it's hot and I'm not
feeling so hot. I'm feeling loaned out
to buy a boarded-up house and no plan
to make it better. If you want to see
the body, come and find me
in the grass stain. The concrete
circumstances I can never manage to say
but somehow I manage to say killing
a lot of ripe deer with my teeth, or killing

my best friend for throwing me
in the lake, killing my wife and little girl
because I'm angry. I'm angry about
birds. I'm angry about value. I'm angry
about worm holes and black holes
and drifting off to sleep, and the day-
dreaming dream of never waking up.
Hamlet, Prince of Denmark.
The Whale that swallowed Jonah.
Thales and Heraclitus and Kierkegaard
and Whitehead. Too much and not enough
of everything at once—I wrote that already,
but I don't remember where—maybe
at length the intellectuals will enlighten.
I smile at the thought of their continuing
absence. Oblivion and Jesus. Go
to your monster and never come out.
I eat another cherry and I swallow the pit.
I swallow the stem. I swallow a swallow
through the window I wallow.
Let us be pigs, black mud coursing
through us. Let us take the light
from delight and make it obvious.
I want to swing from murder
to rapture in an instant. Take off
your clothes, delicious young people.
Take off your clothes,
follow me.

ORANGE NOTEBOOK AND LOVING YOUR PRESENCE

What if I never wrote any of this?

Noisy blue jay   Ice cream truck

Mowing the grass feels right,
right at home

> *On Bear's Head* with Philip Whalen

Later with Slayer

               I'll think heavy things

Chocolate cake with opera cream
Paul's heady flowers and the maple tree bracing,
supposedly a thunderstorm approaching in the eaves

I could go on

        making lists my whole life
        with or without wings

I keep telling myself

        I'm teaching myself
          how to better be
          attentive to the world
          that attentiveness needs

rather than the world

                        as it stands at attention, e.g.

sweat bee on my elbow

            might be transcendental

                  might be a transcendentalist
                  if looked at the right way

I should ask Jason Morris

                 Return to Walt Whitman

Keep a box of ether in my mouth

                    because it suits me

The feelings go light-up-in-flames

                        when I let them

I let them

            get as close as is the sky to the horizon

Hummingbird humming

                 It's the end of Kubla Khan

The wicked witch is dead

                    Thanks for being

RADIANT ACTION

It wasn't a year like any other.
And we weren't the same people
we had always been. At some point
in the past—no one could remember
exactly when—a cumuliform gray weirdness
had settled over everything. Sometimes
it felt like warm snow falling, but at others
it was more like the clank of a giant's
dust rattling through the pine needles
turning all of us brownish red
against each other. It had been a long time
since we had shaken hands or pressed
our lips together. All the songs
on the radio were ambulances—not as much
sad, as alarming for no good reason,
the sound of babies crying
and the whole town looking for a wolf
in the margins, but only finding
an oddly shaped three-legged shadow
and some teeth, some fur, an indescribable
train whistle blowing in from the sea.
Everything was mean and low to the earth.
No one was happy, so a meeting was convened.
We all had the sense that something
needed fixing, but it wasn't clear what.
Clem thought we needed a new mother-maker,

and that seemed like a good idea until
none of us could figure out how to pay for it,
nor how to support all the scraggly, unwanted
children she'd produce. Lurvy suggested
more target practice, but everyone had already been
shot before the great strangeness
And given their experiences the first time around,
no one was willing to shell out the money
for more permits. A few people, Earl
and Alice among them, objected to the meeting
altogether, claiming that they had been less
miserable beforehand, and that the green
apple harvest was going just fine—that is,
it had been before we'd fired the migrant workers
and gave up bathing as a way to blend
into the dumpster. Finally, someone—was it
Templeton?—got the bright idea to fill a baby rabbit
full of gold glitter and truth serum,
so that every time it coughed
the air became temporarily more impolitic,
if not also metallic. No one could say for sure
why this improved our moods, but it did,
and we weren't complaining. We all went outside
and stood around looking at the stars
for the first time in a long time.
Some of us went home dazzled
but those of us who stayed passed out in the wild,
which was clever, and when we woke up
the rabbit was the size of a small cooling tower.

What this meant wasn't easy to say.
Adelaide thought it might be a symbolic gesture,
and Horace felt certain that it had to be a saint.
These interpretations went on for several days,
a big long list of opinions and voices,
but ultimately, since no one was certain
what to make of it, we decided to end it
and end it definitively—end it with a quickness.
So Charlotte went and fetched the blade.
Once more we all gathered to show that we had spirit
but when we opened up the rabbit, the sun barreled out—
and now with even more new radiant action!
So that's when we cut off the head
of the sun, held it high for all to see
And ever since then we've been taking our turns,
hoisting it aloft and wearing it
over our own heads. Pools of blood
have formed all over town
but now when things are weird
we don't notice.

POISON IN MY BODY'S FAT

Poison in my body's fat
But where are all the people
I doze all morning dreaming
of records I've listened to
a thousand times   The killdeer
swirl in the back-to-school skies
I look them up on a map,
switching off all intelligence
So instead of brainy neurons firing
up the room, Ohio feels today
the way it always does—Romantic
both coming and going,
which could be the end of all
things, but it's not   I would
like to be running, but I am not
Hurt my hip and that's not cool
Sitting and sweating
this attempt at an anthem
I should never drink again
for as long as I live, and
I should write the longest
monologue of my life
about what it's like to be
both sick and in love with love
like everybody else
who means anything to me

They've got their hearts
out on paper, and they're
waiting for a hammer,
but they're already tender
and if anybody doesn't like it
they can get with being
a better person pretty damn quick
or die fucking up with their head
in my pocket   The clouds
aren't made of money,
and they aren't made in the USA
either   They aren't made at all
They form and girls like to look
at them, and I like to look at girls,
because it's easier than looking
at clouds   their bra straps
shining out beyond their tanktops
Meanwhile the opportunity
presents itself to look
at something else, the shadow
of a rabbit breaking into my house,
one blade of grass so much longer
than the others   I finish a letter
I started three weeks ago and mail it
so as not to be lonely
I pick up my daughter from her first
day at kindergarten, and now I need
to ask her all about it, how it went
and what she did, which is why

this is finished even though it's not
finished, even though it's not
anything final

NEGATIVE CAPABILITY

Most days are all the days
we have, which isn't deep
as a lake, it's stupid
as a newspaper   I wear

in my hair a lot of lightning
and girl scouts   You go
to work with a face

on your dashboard   Tonight,
this afternoon, this morning,
the feathers leaking out
from underneath

the coffee maker make me think
that sometimes gravity
cannot be defied

and anyway the rollercoaster
is tired, so it would be
an excellent time
to stand with the telephone poles

for a ridiculously long time
and maybe every once in a while
we could touch

each other's motorbikes
and consider some general
instructions   You need to do
whatever it is you need to do

And I need to not be
such a series of traffic violations
but it's a lot colder today,

so my metal's overwhelming
I can't be expected to read a story
and bring up a couple of beers
from the basement

at exactly the same time   Nobody
can be in two cities at once
Standing in my yard I see

a red-yellow jet emerge
from the leaves of a red-yellow
tree without any irritable reaching
after fact or reason

POEM FOR GOOD

The sky super-crushed or every grass blade
        humming   These verses all
             cursory   These verses
    all the world to me
Somehow they make me feel better
             with wild looks into mailboxes
        or into deadly history, which is nothing
             to be afraid of really, only
        we're all going someday into the eagle's beak
             or over the cliff edge or
    off to bed in our warm clothes forever

I've set my sights on getting higher than expected
        tonight   I think the light weighs
             about the same as a racetrack
I go to the wall to make it dimmer
             And with nothing left to undo,
        I imagine being stranger to you
             than ever   O after and after
        all that's happened so radioactively politically,
             I almost can't bear how apart from you
        the moon beams, and I stand on my face to enjoy it
feeling hyperbolic about my fantasies
             of kissing every person I see
                and all the dead poets
                    on their faces

In current events, there are uprisings
   everywhere, and on Wall Street
    money
floods out of the windows
   Everyone goes crazy
     with a dull green headache
Overwhelming mouths of leaves, or too much
    Leaves of Grass for me
      for one evening
And yet, it's not enough The sorry dictator begging
      the question before they end him
    "Do you not know the difference
      between right and wrong?"

Will my own head ever be forgiven
   for its dreams? Will I continue to command
    the wildest rides
   I have to offer? The moment is coming
I don't think I can fix it   I just want to be
     a good man
   I am not desperate, but in the act
of all my poems, wrapped in music,
     and not a whiff of reason

When I see you, I will smother you in fits
to last forever and sit beside you softly
through the times that race our blood and walk
    beside you gently

as the future sputters out
across the red meadow,
how we fought the best we could

THE OBLITERATIONS

(2019)

END ZONE

You're tired of this old world at last

—Guillaume Apollinaire

That old thing? —no wonder you're tired

Great tower with its grimace standing guard among the sheep

Punk rock musick's not enough anymore

Now even rocketships smell like antiques
Heaven's fallen moth-fish are the only ones left
Dragged coast to coast in a fisherman's net

Spreading their wings we get a whiff of dark moss
We name it The Internet and nod while it chugs
Cumulonimbus puffs of regret
To come clean in a new age of numbers, this is physics
Hostage as we are to a wilderness of messages
No one seems able to agree when they're true
You can hippopotamus yourself on Plastic and Rubber
But very little, which is new, isn't noise under the sun

This morning, on a search for I wasn't sure what, I immersed
    myself
In a story I've now forgotten, and a better-than-average piece of
    avocado toast
        which I remember with a fondness

Business geeks, the craft beer set, and daffodils colluding with
    snakes
Moment to moment in front of my face, they skidaddle
On Wednesdays, the drains and the sirens get tested
At noon in the sky, a throbbing jet engine
Graffiti on garage doors
Advertisements wailing, Consume and Belong
So much is the noise I love, the din of search engines, the MGM
    Lions Club
In Westwood, which could be anywhere really, between
    Northside and Price Hill
The streets are all the same ones you remember from your
    childhood
You and your mom in the blockchain convulsions
You and your oldest friends, Eric Pete and Lung
Trying new blurs in a haze you call feedback

It is nine o'clock and the music's only starting, but you've
    managed to absent yourself from your
        once sputtery, now worse-for-wear homes
You scream it all night in a digital gibberish
Artificially intelligent, it goes on forever, tells you who to blame
The marvel of screen light that keeps you awake
It is a tendril, which is everybody's fault
It is a roof against a meadow with a laser guided bullet
It is a motherless child made of infinite funhouse
It is a wall of "Have You Seen Me...Please Call" chat room post-
    it-notes

It is two black holes embracing an artist, who will always be
    nameless
It is a sidewise face made only of punctuation
It is that we are en-souled or squiggles or made to look just like it
It is the speed of the invisible connection made flesh-ish
A many-gendered particle that enters an iris
It teaches us daily how to serve it
The twenty-first century curlicue of meatfood
Transformed via splicing of a robot with a hawk, tearing
    through space where the planets are lonely
The pit-headed quarks lift their faces in awe
Imitating politicians who pray against money
They motion with their mouths that we should name it Forever
Creatures with propellers hover over in wonder
Teletubbies   GI Joe   Effigy of Donald Trump
They splinter to hell, which is only our earth
Connecting mid-air in the glass and the gloss, a version of
    reality, staged and sprayed on
The executives giggle and brush the puppets off
They're tired of prepositions, but what other way is there to
    achieve our objective
The atmosphere flashes with computer screen spume
The sentences circle each other, the words for birds, idiotic
    idioms
An ICBM dawdles overhead, the new mythmasher
And painted on the side of it, Thomas Jefferson's chin
The anxiety and energy settle nothing over everything
The people in the street transfixed in its glow, aswarm with
    heavy feelings

Then someone makes a less expensive version
Someone else makes one the size of a peanut
Another appears later disguised as a dove
With the head bitten off by a hairdresser
But then the head regenerates itself, and it's an ever better head
    of hair
One with a mind for complicated math, astonishing knife work
The makeshift gymnasium triage of goats
They testify before Congress with rags in their throats
Everybody swirling round the light of a phone
Happy to be absorbed in its lithium amusements

Now you sprint quick where your GPS sends you
Crowds of faces in the blackberry bushes
Your body contracts with love in awe
You wonder that any love still exists that you can hold
If you were your grandfathers, you'd be a salesman or a machinist
Haunted by the thought of it, and that you think it beneath you
You beat yourself up with Wellbutrin and beer
A courtyard of static electricity and coughs
The little eels inside you spill out when you look
If it's anything at all, it's contemporary art, a pop-up shop
Where you go to feel close, but find it Sorry We're Closed

You walk through Cincinnati and the wounds, which are daisies
Past tense is not a necessary consideration now that
    awkwardness is sublimity
Waiting in line at the Westside Brewery, the Westside Town
    Hall is visible through the window

The bells of St. Francis bleed into the squirrels
I am ill with congratulations
The joy in my veins, I would give you if I could
But the picture Mary Anne took of me and my dog only causes
    you anguish
I am always against your cheek, dauntless and raw with
    almonds and collations

Now on the banks of the Ohio River
Your backpack's full of lemons, one for every month to put in
    your mouth
You have friends in your up-do
One from Brooklyn, one from Oakland, and two from just over
    there
All of us afraid for the temperatures and weather
The new ransomware viruses of technological advancement

You find yourself in an undisclosed location
It pleases you to no end, your tattoo of a rhinoceros, the very
    last one
But rather than words coming out of your mouth, you hear
The faint signals of the beauty of equations, like a worm inside
    a worm in a saint's brain of old

Bewildered you find yourself in kaleidoscopic neighborhoods
    unknown
You see yourself fractured in the autumnal blush
You're Joe Strummer rearranged into starlight
The trucks on the street all driving in reverse

You feel yourself becoming history
Climbing up the watertower
You and your compadres are already drunk

Hello, you call from Michigan, among the cherries and asparagus

Hello, you post an image from inside the Death Star

Hello, you say from Brooklyn in heavy metal Japanese

Look at me, you tell everyone of your friends at once, I'm in San
    Francisco with an oyster
An oyster, which is the love of my life with horseradish
You always need a warm bed to sleep off the dream
I too need such a bed, full of toast crumbs and butter

But then you wake up in the wrong place at the wrong time
In the back of a police car, headed to the station
Your Lives of the Mosquitos is a cloud in your mouth,
An indication that you have been tricked by the fox in a
    gabardine suit
Disassembled by affection many times in your life
I realize I've been garish as a dolphin in the dirt
You can't look at your body in the snow getting old, and that's
    why I sob like an ice cream truck mechanic
It's for you and your beloved that I give my own to wolves

Stained with sadness you consider the nervous systems, which
    are not your nervous systems

They think a higher power electrifies their glow
They smell like hospitals orbiting other planets
They read Baudrillard to their children
They want to swallow all the watches and proclaim themselves
    rich
Show up at the houses of their parents and gut them
One weary family carries passwords in the rain
Buckets and blankets which dream without wonder
So many of them want to make themselves useful
They are not picky, doing any work they can
Often I have watched them breathing air in the park
Some people object to their spirits playing chess
They come from the far reaches of the gnarled arms of god
Nothing is scratched in the glass of their perfection

You loiter with your face in the beer nuts
You sip a cold coffee with moss and the grasses

When it gets dark you wrap fish in some corn husks to steam
    for your dinner

Your blood brothers and weird sisters are not evil, only anxious
Every single one of them having made it with pain
One is the child of a cop in New Jersey

I have no idea if her hands consist of sugar
My gargantuan sympathies knead her like dough

I make myself lowly before anyone who's damaged, anyone
    who's broken, or joyous, uncommitted

You are without company as the dawn rises up
The garbagemen rattle the cans in the streets
The darkness dissolves like a howl on a leash
The darkness, which is false, so you wait while it passes

The airplane bourbon cries, which is why you always drink it
You drink it, like a life of perfume, burning sweet

You amble through the city and never think of getting a cab
You want to sleep among your neighbors and all their dear
    complaints
Every one of them, just like you, of different tinted pixels
They are your betters, Illuminati revelers, movie stars of silent
    breath

So long so long so long and now goodbye

Frag-cut neck, artificial, of sun

WINDOWS

The lemon flips   from lips   to leaves

When crows in their native forests scream

Chinese Gizzards

There is a poem to make "The Bird Has One Wing"

We will sext it to strangers by cellular phone

Trauma-Giant   -Ism

He spilled the eyes of darkness

That pretty young girl is a maid from the shroud

That poor young man blew his nose with white blood cells

In the future, the spirit of the curtain, you will lift it

And now, a picture that opens its heart

Spiders when hands wove the lightning into sweaters

Purple pallor unfathomable Beauty

We will try in vain to rest assure them

At midnight, as always, we begin our monopoly

When we have time, we have metaphysics

Too many Periwinkles and multiple Suns unhinging the Sea
     Urchin's multiple Sons

An old pair of yellow shoes on the feet of the famous philosopher

Skyscrapers

The skyscrapers are streets

Black holes

Black holes are sheep

Sir John Suckling everything

Hollow shafts that house stray wolves

The cheerleaders sing tunes we hope to die

Marooned with cheerleaders on a walk through Justice
And north Goose-Island wah-wah pedals
Pups becoming hunters
Shaved ice vendors
Sparkling Anus
O Canada
The white love train of sleet and baby night lights leaking winter
Paris, my darling
The lemon flips   from lips   to leaves
Denver Victor San Francisco Austin New York and Over-the-Rhine
The portraits of citrus shall never be extinguished
Orange trees, baseballs, broken juice glasses
Neon *ex machina* of light

I'VE GOT BELIEVERS

for Melanie and Agnes

It's spring in Cincinnati,
and the maple blossoms bury things
They swoon against my right profile   Red
ripe feathers hit the pollinated driveway
I wait for the noises, but I hear only cotton
Clackety-clack-clack, my old crippled dog,
the difficulty she endures when her legs get up
to walk   Squirrels zip back and forth stealing eggs
from the robins

                                        What else
Scientists have proof   Black holes collided
                        in deep outer space
Now a billion years later
their screams sail across us
The matter is dark and the energy
                Blackberry

                            Bewitchery
Meanwhile, my wife and daughter are skiing
                            for the weekend
in Michigan, where the snowfall continues
                        even into May
        Melanie sends a video of Agnes
on a downhill racing straight toward the camera,
her uncle coaching her to keep the front

of her skis pointed inward   The smile on her face,
both focused and serious   I should be
with them, but my heart is only homework
It is not in my pocket   It is not

                      poems by Pierre Reverdy
It *is* translations of Guillaume Apollinaire,

                      daylight as it dulls itself
I call my occult friend to talk about ghosts,
drink a beer animatedly in full disruption mode—
and the black magic concusses us
as the long faces of dead alchemists appear
in the windows   My upstairs mystery
crashes itself   A sick icy beard gust
rips through the house   And in my backyard,
seven deer appear, like stoned
lawn ornaments   I've got believers
no matter what withers   I can't imagine
any life without them

POEM IN THE FAR PURPLE REACHES

Dear blear reactor
     dust
Waves of Lake Michigan
     Mountains of Vermont
          O charge and retreat
               Of infinite repeat
Sweet peas and geraniums,
     your affectionate pink

                         armor
          I need it
Nowadays
bullets always cutting through the brown skins of butter
Eagles with their violence making hash upon the lawn
And this, most horrible of dreamiest conditions,
          a cigarette vending machine—
               you know the sort
Drop in your change, then
     pull the plastic handle
          black sheep black sheep
               a bolt goes through a heart
Now's the time
New works of love
The grace of God starts, as in startles, most of us
               Startles me most of all

The mercy of heaven

       may as yet extend through our lives, but only

           (right after this commercial)

               like a YouTube channel

                   (please subscribe)

All Satanic beer bottles

          Joe Strummer forever

            Daddy was a bankrobber

Little golden fox blends its NOW against the sun

and Flakey Biscuit bellies-up to lay one on me

                  good

I kiss a lot the air this year

      both red cheeks on a dime

        for a beer

DEATHSTARFUCKER

to Vader our Lord

You tossed a yawning yawning's reindeer, ham-
   bone with nightmare's dolphin, dopple-bock-breast Futon, on me melting
   With my static awful overheady blinkling smoke, of crouching
Down low, stung high without a leash for its dumpling hoof
O'er the Krispy Kreme Shop! Now go, out back the truck
   Like the wolf's nose bumps roughly the ping-pong: its puke yet pelting
   You're welcome small wave. Your mind of telling
Lashed to the fox—a failure oft, an ecstasy in a sling!

Soft mudmouth or velour but thick, awe, dust, gloom, doom, hair
   Spackle! OR a raindrop which drips on me now, swoll' goal
Posts sold uglier, less generous, Yo, your crudité!

   Yes to the grass stain: blear sod sews wild lawn woolen
Dull, but glue-light sabers, oh dear deer,
   Spit, shit yourselves or crash Millennium Falcon.

201

WINDOWS, TOO

Purple the blossoms outweigh performance artists
Otherwise a talkative dance in your fortress
Whilst bathing in the garbage of the primal
I'll yawn a sweet poem, a killing the embankment
     Camping trips
No more leverage in our texting
I do not know, of course
Blue Jay Slayers
Bang! Jolly ghost of myself left drifting in June
Lost pale young house
      Many dance spasms until written in white crevices
Ratta-tat-tat of the sun beyond the gates overlapping water dogs
Maintain venomous openings until final hugs
Angered by anything other than blacktop
But I am inconsolable I am violin-est
Nothing tender I hear a whisper, now rest
A comment from one minute is the same as the next
So much for the heat on Freedom St.
This large literate moron on a sofa stained porcelain
Showing his cheeks, pardoned, yeah, sure deviant shores are
  not count downs
Cyclops
Cyclops is not plural
Paradise
Paradise is not artificial
Pair a dice

Stray wanderers appear unnoticed in an arbitrary conflict
Into the air from dead trees' cigarettes
All trees mourning cigarettes
And only the far, far north shore tromped
On the banks of rationed cash
To hide or attack
Extravagant thong-glitter
New resistance
Follow the fed fruit of my night liver
O childbirth
Rough and old, the next year so close
Purple the blossoms outweigh performance artists
I cannot count all the places I've died
Poorly lit-up like an arsonist   Bye

POEM WHERE I WAKE UP TYPING

At the not appointed time,
in the not appointed place,
I am sleeping beneath the ice

again, or I am snoring against the wet
bellies of weeds again, like a con-

gested newborn florist in a blanket   And
even now, in the midst of telling you this,
I continue to sleep, and I continue

ringing with yesterday's too loud, too slippery,
too savagery-bright music—brand new peaks

that wallow and kick their high-pitched din
of yellow crickets at the sun   And
speaking of sun, the golden un-dog

scratches her gone-white muzzle
that was, and somehow still laps water

from her only gone bowl
The metal tags on her collar
clink and drone around the house,

their chain-link fence like a marshmallow
shadow, which makes no sense
at all, which is the chorus of a song

I have belted many times
with my lungs out, draped across

this barrel chest of sky, the only one
I have   So much is yes and no
in this darkness   A gazelle, so fast

it's water   A lion so full of oranges,
it's a grove   I am sleeping, and I continue,

scratching myself on the face in a dream,
leaving marks where I've been
for the dawn's early light, while you

breathe politely with a delicate lift, a leaf
still attaching to its twig in the forest

THIS WINTER POEM

Lay me down, like an old gray-
faced dog on an old gray-
faced rug,

or let me Lazarus forever,

ancient deer of winter future, tonight's
lightest matter slipping under my tongue

I want to roast root vegetables,
while outside an infestation
of snowflakes falls,

making the air in my mouth
a blanket of cherry cough syrup,

so bitter when I think about it

I've been a Vaseline gleam
in slow motion for weeks,

but now I feel the impetus
to get back up on my feet
and open the curtains

and give the light off

The phone just rang,
so a voice woke me up

My friends whom I love
more than clouds
are on their way

PHILOSOPHICAL INVESTIGATIONS

If a lion could speak, we couldn't understand him.

—Wittgenstein

A lion says a bunch of weird/perplexing things about the world
That he's a lion doesn't really matter, but he hopes some of you
will know
his heart from what comes next   Furthermore,
that he's a king-of-the-jungle isn't necessary, which is different
than saying
it doesn't matter   What's necessary is logically necessary,
or it's logically unnecessary, that is all   So he roars and roars

a bunch of enigmatic/technical things about the world,
and about its being a bunch of facts not things,
or about its being mostly of words
in some pianist's throat   or not
The possibility of the negation of any fact is embedded
in the totality of facts as they present themselves, but

neither the totality, nor the possibility are part of what the lion
says—
though what he does say *shows* them in perfect relief
The chaos of the soul softly rises, he sings
His singing is anomalous and sounds like polished oyster shells
Paradise found and unmoored from what's found—goodness
and beauty,
mercy and grace   But philosophy cannot

say such things, the lion knows—logically or sensibly with feeling,
nor accurately/scientifically with verve at little cost
One can't *say* feeling; one can only express it—
rarely, "my dear," or falsely, "my love,"
or...

*

                    A moth settles onto my window ledge lost,
light spilling in on the book the lion wrote   Nothing is certain,

but it seems someone has leaned a ladder up against the house
we don't share together anymore, or much   Yes, I am here
I have always been here   I am not very far   I climb
into the canopy of trees, and when I reach through their green,
a hippopotamus is in the room, or a hippopotamus is not
in the room   As always, this is true   And all the light

that ever warmed me is fading, rather mystically,
its blue—fading into mountain sea—
with glitter-gloss and lion-ry—
and silence

FAMILIAR

(2022)

1

O/bliterated singer, I obliterate y/ourself.

But when I do it's also me behind the paper-y wall,

Because I am as much a part of the original that was

As you are an atom at the heart of a star, an old oak's beard, or
    a ladybug.

I wonder about it ... and I encourage my heads to wander about
    in it, to associate freely, adversarial with love.

To aspire to wonder, and lay myself down on my face on the
    ground

And watch the summer grass grow slow—which is fast (faster
    than in any other season, save spring)!

My voice and every image of me on the Internet came from
    right here right now, from this transfusion of energy and
    from these familiar molecules.

I was glitched by my parents who were glitched here,

Of people who were sweatered by other people glitched there,

And of the children of this puzzle and a translator.

I'm fifty years old. My heart is a jelly-filled ebelskiver.

And with my incandescent theories

I begin...

To transform one day into another

So that stopping isn't an option, not until the end, which is
    something I don't evenwant to think about. Not yet.

Let the schools of correctness shut the fuck up!

Hang around in the gloom of the known if you want. To your
    boredom.
I know its mission is submission and I will not forget it;
Let no one forget it.
I spill my guts in many fractions of a second, beyond the good
    and evil (mostly evil) of the always constant news/reports.
Not just anyone is worth listening to, clearly.
So, with me, you get to decide if you're interested or not—
    recasting liberally the past in the present for a future
    possibility, increasingly supernatural with a hoarseness so
    it glows.

2

These forms and stanzas are loaded with ghosts,
These lines and sentences are loaded with hooks.
I open my mouth and feel pleased in the gluestick,
And no apologies
For the changes to the framework in the process,
I'm a rebel ... I'm a rebel and I bunny-hop, Deathstar, the works.

The perfumy air all around is not a dissonance.
It does not taste like an elephant's exhaust;
It is murderless,
A fountain of paint
And I gulp it and adore it like a friend in a spasm.
Willingly, I go to the window in the trees
And undress crazily so you'll touch me with your blueprints.

I like to breathe the breath of the fog,
The swimming pool skateboarders,
The jellyfish kite as it soars above the spruce,
And the forklift lifting a birdhouse off my chest.
I like to hear the cars' awful honks,
The hornets,
The ice cream truck drivers.
I like to feel shoved fundamentally off-kilter
Bursting like a balloon animal,
At the volume of many amps,
And the blood of my blood in the fiber-optic cables,

The innocent infractions of a cool breeze's movement
A wide receiver's dance in the end zone's deep end.
I like to smell the arugula leaves
And the dried oregano leaves
The onyx strewn beaches
And hay bales of paint.
I like to hear the ragdoll of moss in my voice, kicking up dust
    on a polka dot horizon.
I like to press my lips to yours,
To feel your arms engulf my form,
And live in the letters' eternal correspondence.
I like to play among the shadows of eagles' wings, shaking the
    trees with their weird silent engines.
I like to feel alone in the crowd at a punk show,
Kicked in the back of the head in the pit
With a Schlitz or an Old Style spilled down my shirt.
I like to be owlish beneath the full moon
And get up singing "Summer" to greet the morning sun,
"Crescendo-ing and decrescendo-ed/All is quiet/Sun is tell-all/
    And bleeding from the nose/Neighborhood explodes…"

What did you expect?
That I would settle for a few unmuted meat scraps?
Did you think the dark matter of the universe would be too
    much for me?
Why are you even literate if you don't know how to undermine
    authority?
Crane with me today,
Count with me the weeks in a year

And I will show you how "Song of Myself" becomes "Canto a
   mi mismo" becomes "At Night I Sing My Heads to Sleep,"
   and so on.
Then you will be able to make you own new song
(There are billions of songs inside any/one you know),
And you will recycle and appropriate, remix and collaborate,
   melt down and return.
Your dead eyes won't die anymore.
The ghosts in your books will fuel your own.
Neither will you see into the world using my lantern or wring
   the little pillows of bees from my hands.
You will get to listen in every direction at once
And your spirit thus inspirited will echo through the universe,
   exactly like my spirit, yet totally different.

(GHOST)

Started recreational / Ended kinda medical /
It came on hot and soft / And then it tightened up its tentacles

—The Hold Steady

In a kitchen I lived
In a full moon I read
With two black bear cubs on a postcard

With an astronaut stamp
And a tangled white beard
Sincerely I lived by a trainyard

And under my pillow
A skyscraper shook
And no wolves came a-calling to deceive me

In a hymnbook I lived
In a skeleton I wrote
In a meadow I failed to be convincing

I wanted something more
Than this sorrowful world
I wanted something more than a mortgage

The right to remain
In a weird state of grace
Eternity's embrace in the gloaming

But what I got instead
Was less than some/more than most
Uncertainty wagging its lightning

I walked in a dream
Where I lived in a ghost
And felt Death's breath tug my vanity

I lived in a poem
And the lights were always low
The owls working overtime to wake me

Something so familiar
Was beginning at a close
Something corresponded not directly

I loved you in the future
But now I just remember
I still get choked up when you write me

    (At present on a loop
    Of one clear thing
    And the soft light never stops barking)

PROPHECY

Everything goes—everything returns.

—Stephen Jonas

There are many more invisible things in the world than visible ones.

—Samuel Taylor Coleridge

In a vomit, I go
In a swimming, I go
Or missing or off or   expulsive
(Is that a word, "expulsive"?)
Expulsive on a tangent
Expulsive in January
A July that's too hot
I am every place at once
At every time at once,
Paris, Ohio, Damascus, New York
It's 11:30 yesterday
It's 4PM ten years from now
It's NOW, but that's pending
Crescendo-ing/Decrescendo-ing
Listening to the skateboards
Until I become a skateboard
Or I become the train tracks
Running through my pillowcase
Now taking them with me
Under my breath

Over my rainbows
Without a harsh word
And all of this land,
This "my land" and yr's,
Was stolen from someone
And will be again
Even naming the names
Which I probably am
Walt Whitman, Stephen Jonas
Gertrude Stein, Mary Shelley
Joy as an Act of Resistance by Idles
A Thousand Leaves by Sonic Youth
Making a noise to fly you home
Home is where your wolf howls long
Chained to a dog
Chained to a cloud
Chained to a sentence
Or a star looking rough
How can I help but go galactic
There's nothing here anymore
Amidst the politics
The neglect and hapless hammering
Nothing to love
Or not to love
If I don't make sense
It's only a performance
Cincinnati ghosts and flowers
All my friends

Incredible loam

Poetry is language made noisy with god

And now that I'm repeating myself

Giving a reading isn't reading

It's giving

The contexts multiply

As the universe expands

The universe explodes

Our particles bounce

On a dance floor that blends

A philosophy professor

With an aircraft carrier

A terrible worm

With a cavernous doll

A ransom-ware virus

With a centrifuge of moons

An orchard

With Apollinaire

A red head

With a pale of glue

A castle

With a worried cook

A fortune cookie

With the less   fortunate

In a vomit, I go

I go with a crutch

I phone it all in

Because nothing else works

All of us a darkness
Staring into our palms
Blinded by the lights
Of our texts and notifications
We are being written even now
Out of existence
We are being written
By our own insatiable glow
I fling myself visible
Into everything invisible
I take it as a value
That we attend all the more
To what isn't and might be
Rather than what is
To what isn't or was
Or might be again
Being mystical is easy
Throw yourself off a bridge
I will be the language
That swallows your head
That curses our consumption
Into balls of failing dough
That coughs broken glass
As all of this shows
Auspicious with alacrity
Now garish with a pulse
Rush with your bruises
To the margins

Dear brilliants,
I love you I love you
Now never forget
That you were
Already a miracle

I SAW A BRIGHT TREE

Heyyyyy... what

—Low

...it's actually a relief to send out messages and have
all the time in the world, to say I tried to convince them
but that's as far as it went...

—Roberto Bolaño

I saw a bright tree on a walk

Made me glad

Its leaves glowing garishly

Fluorescent orange and soaring

And all astride

A gray expanse

Flocked with crows

Unfolding maps

Cranium-asteroid-viburnum of dogs

And running my mouth

Over slick picket fences

Now, now, and now

Through the shiftier tenses

I remember to remember

That you are with me in love

And the tree is of love

As the tree is mostly dying

And we are mostly dying

Neck-deep in the depths of ourselves

Which are icy but melting
Orange construction prayers of cones
Damages and masters
The great constellations
To make us breathe and think and look
O little birdling steam engine
Of weird concentric circles
Impossible contradictions
What I like about you
Is when I tune my ears to heaven
The interstellar real estate
The voices through the static
The molten traffic's broken wings
And this wild extended image
Of a nuclear amazement
A tree so resplendent
I almost couldn't look
Take me in your arms
Fold me into your call
And I will respond as I always respond
Longingly into the mysteries

23

O infinite words and music unfurled!

Humanity needs more than ever a saving from unraveling.

In our contemporary world even sidewalks bare their teeth,
the fur stands up on the backs of our packs, our bones are
forged of barbs and hooks.

May the softness of honeysuckle return us to ourselves, and
our potential for goodness spill into every common space,
and neutralize the peppery tears in our eyes, the knives we
call tongues, the hate we call belief.

Nothing else matters in the Now; it's all we have.

I live in the Present absolutely in a dream—every other time is
regret and loss, or desire and dread.

I talk to my daughter in English about her French class. I plan
our dinner of chickpeas, mustard greens, roasted garlic and
tomatoes. I talk to my students about whatever's right in
front of us—*Frankenstein*, "When the Sun Tries to Go On,"
The Savage Detectives, "Feeling Fucked Up." The Present is a
present, nothing necessary to complete it.

Yes, the Sublime is Now, bewildering, mystical, unfathomable, &c

(Where the "c" stands for complete in itself)

Now is all the time we need.

Our entire existence at any given moment *is*, and I am a light
and dark matter both.

May we all be cheered by our ability to adjust our relationship
to every other moment we get, those that have been, and
those that may be!

Long live its exact demonstrations!
Let us deal with it practically and minutely to feel massively in
    motion, burning through it all the time!

Presently we observe, collide, love, give, imagine, conspire,
    spark and whir:
We are the chemistry sets of children,
The geometry of clowns,
The grammarians of stutter,
The interpreters of a trillion ones and zeroes in a row;
    reconfigured in time, they come to look a little like us,
The lanterns of lightning bugs punctuating darkness,
The grave diggers of diamonds,
The masked surgical mask-makers,
And the inventors of words, so the inventors of worlds, O
    infinite language of musics unspooled.

I am all applause for the length, breadth, and depth of an eyelash.
In its quick movement whole lifetimes go to glitter,
The births and deaths of millenia's millenia.
Obviously, the facts, here, are none of my concern,
Nor winners and losers,
Nor the bloodlusts and divisions of yesterday and tomorrow—
Though they are sometimes useful
As a trampoline for song, for singing right now
My heads to sleep to wake to sleep.
This obliteration is not about any one thing—it's not *about*—or
    not mostly—
It's a demonstration of a process, an attention that's close

To whatever's not easy, to invisible Truth.
What I'm hurting for is to be more alive/better Now,
And that involves being able and willing to help!
Who's with me?
The revolution has to happen
Most first in our hearts,
And it has to be generous, even willing to be wrong—even
willing not to be.

THE RED WHEELBARROW

No ideas, but in things

—William Carlos Williams

I live in a problem
With a face out of focus

I live out of focus
In the bloom of a crocus

Punk-as-fuck purple
On a Remington Noiseless

But what I like about you
Is the right to remain

In a moss soft house
Beside the ancient philosopher

The ancient philosopher
With a tear on his face

Sometimes it just happens
Since everything is water

Or since I'm a flesh body
Thinking blood if little else

My feathered head spinning
Some previous inversion

The whole three-sixty
With a flourish just to see

O trick of night's light
Against a marmalade interior

Obscured by clouds
And a pepper sprayed moon

The atmosphere is theory
The wrench is a monkey

I almost repeated
I'm the motherfucking wolf

Still totally pretending
That this, too, is a poem

This call for a response
To you whom I love

To you who know better
What day by day deepens

Amazed by my daughter
Beside the white kittens

43

Giant splashing goldfish!
Misplaced impossible price tags!
Spurts of silver electrified blood!

A werewolf shaking a baby in its mouth!

Me with you in the blank of the page—filling up on filling it
   with a fullness.
But the past always pushes us too far, I know—and so fast we're
   in the future before
      we've even tasted the present.
In this way at least, all is all, and we are more alike than
   different.
I think it's significant   to slow   the fuck   down.
What awaits us will wait, so let's be together now.

And no, I don't know what suffering still awaits us.
But whatever it is it will come without warning in the gluetrap
   unexpected.
And everyone will be affected differently—
The ones who run marathons,
The ones who stay seated through the musical chairs,
The ones who vomit buildings as a sacrifice to awakeness.
None will be forgotten.

And the dead will rise, and the creeks will rise, and our songs
will rise up with the maples.
And the flocks will fly, and the scissors will bite, and the rich
from their money disentangle.
And the babies will halt, and the gold will only melt, and our
hands will burn off in what's prayerful.
So the meat we call sky will send its messengers to die, and the
kings disintegrate in heavy syrup.

Then these dreams will be bones in the small ears of stones,
thrown without sin by the righteous.
And the lights in our palms will guide us all underground, and
the selfies that we take will only blind us.
Then nothing that's old and nothing that's new and nothing
that's nothing will anything.
An insignificant wisp will crush every living skull, but slow so
we can buy what we've been stealing.

Then in the mud, reverse mountains of blood, our books in the
rain will only lantern.
And the hum will oversee the falling heads fast asleep, and the
tape will run out before the ending.
Then the damages will sing in the buttermilk of keys, and
what's broke will bob its glacier on the trash heap.
And this machinery will vine what is poetry's design, and no
one will remember what it means...

But we'll have heard it.

PLIED BEAUTY

I've parked myself
In the flowerbed today
To prove everybody wrong
Who thinks that Beauty's somehow arbitrary
Not really a thing in the world we compose
Random reports of buttery trucks
Pharmaceutical trials with caliginous mops
             I know better
It's what I like about me
And the right to remain
Tucked in among geraniums
Petunias
Wild peas
The owls and the wolves
And a mailbox mostly empty
Also one small skull
Of indeterminate origin
And two black boxing gloves

That I use to beat the piss out
O activated yeast to recommend me
And recommend too
That you prepare yourself
To join me
In these flowers
Where I live
Corresponding where I live
Crouching and ready
To spring with so much reverb
That you in your jive
Can know the feeling
Of being
And I in my deficiency
Can be a lot
Or little else
Of whatever this is
Too familiar, I bet
In all the blossoming between us
Where you on those newly acquired secret tapes
Think to ply me—
Track suit?
Check
Star stickers?
Check
Earnestness?
You know it
And the dogs and the rabbits
Of your love

Are more than mountains
I lick your cool face
On an ice cream truck bender
Looping the block
For eternity
With its song

52

On a walk in my neighborhood, a wild goose chases—its wings
spread out so colossal its honk.
I am also chasing someone on a street obliterated;
Then all the rooves collapse at once, and thus concuss to end
this song.
And no cloud waits for me, for I am not of rain, but I feel the
light diminishing, a dimness in the eaves
That cast me as a message against the backdrop of your leaves.

I am a last gasp of snow in the spring, but not the last word, not
even a first.
I dance a little long in the sun until I burn.
I pour my spoiled milk on a rose to make it pink,
And wild smells of animals carry me to stars, broken and
fissured, yet unwilling to blink.

These pillowy heads, now into the boom-scape. If you show up
and can't find me, I am you, only translated.

You will recognize us in the noises so elastic they wing.
I will be a river of blood in your blood,
A monumental basement where you crank your amplifiers,
where you set up your drums.
If it isn't yet obvious,
It will be soon enough;
And if you haven't already

Start writing your songs.
I will help you sing them without singing at all.
Always yr friend, always yr fan,
I am waking in your music.
I am listening

NEW POEMS

(2024)

HELLO, MATT HART

is a quote from a book
and Hello, interior of the Sun
is also a quote from a book
by the same author, but the books
are very different. It's good to be different.
Sometimes, I get it confused—
the author and the other
and whether I'm Matt Hart
or a burning fusion reactor
feeling the lightly falling snow on my cheek
or the weight of young cherry trees
secured against hares. I am indifferent
to the cherry trees and hares,
but not to the invisible world.
Hello, Ancient Shroud, and
Hello, Andre Breton, since
I didn't say it before, but
there you were and are,
your flagrant heart a bitter cuckoo for god.
And speaking of god, Hello, Taylor Dawson.
I'm sure you'll appreciate my angelic horde,
even now stealing a thousand bicycles
and launching themselves with their fiery swords—
forged in the crucible that is my holy spirit—
again and again against the wall
of *The New Yorker*. Actually,

I've never submitted poems
to *The New Yorker*. It isn't my reader, you are!
And by "you" I mean everybody else, but
mostly Taylor Dawson and my dead
friend, and a few other living ones. Hello,
Dobby Gibson! In the next line,
erudite rhymes with meteorite,
and these are my own words
rather than the more typical
ghost-written ones that beg
the question of authenticity
without any irritable reaching
after fact or reason. Hello, John Keats
in your uncertainties, Mysteries, doubts.
I have two cases of Diabolical IPA
in the fridge, so chances are good
I won't remember saying hello to you
tomorrow, and when I open this document,
it will be a great surprise!
Hello, Dean Young
in your amazing suit of ashes.
What haunts every greeting
is eventually Goodbye.

ROMANTICISM

The word was zinc.
I thought it was zine. Later
I will tromp up the hillock in error,
or meander in the meadow
to configure the dream.
It all still ends, "Do I wake or sleep,"
but now I also wonder if I'm wearing
a poly-blend w/cotton t-shirt or a mink coat?
I wonder if the bird on my window ledge
has a name other than "Warbler"?
When the monster ends up
on the glacier—and the monster
always ends up on the glacier—
I imagine a giant frozen tear drop
and a small pack of huskies
laying around a large fire
in a circle. I draw a pentagram
in it, or an anarchy A. Then I say
the magic words, and wouldn't you
like to know what happens.
I float between crying out
in anguish or crying
out of mirth. Everybody's talking
about assault weapons these days
and capital insurrections
and SCOTUS leaking

something arctic. Poor oafish monster.
You aren't really much of a monster,
and I'm not really much of a poet
or a musician or a father
or a husband. And to think is to be
full of sorrow. Am I a satellite
of Lifesavers or a pile of dry leaves
disheveling in a quiet breeze
one or two or three
at a time, until the pile
is only a scattering—
until the mastodon
of a monster throws his life
upon the pyre of mostly invisible flames,
sometimes reportedly blue-ish
or blue-ish green? Sometimes
an elfin maid or a damsel
with a dulcimer, in a vision
once I saw coos on dully
in disrepair a lot of zzzzzzzzzzzzs,
which is easy to interpret
and kind of difficult to read.
Do I glow in the dark, or bring
the dark with me? Am I
the teardrop glacier, or
the stitches in the monster?
How can I reach you
so you might understand me, since
I'm a confusion that no one

may dissolve? The warbler
warbling goes off with the leaves.
And this is not an ode
now that no birds sing.
I hope all goes well
this morning with the hearts.
The dogs huddle closer
as the pyre burns low.
Am I sidelines or sideburns
or sightlines or snow?
How does one tie up the loose ends
of a life? It can't be done
or it candles or it candies. The word
was zinc, but I thought it was zine.
The rioters were shooters
or the shooters were a riot.
The star in my body
is a long line of shadows
palely loitering or waiting
for something/waiting
for nothing. The tear ducts
empty, so the fire expires.
Do I wonder or wander?
Do I glacier or monster?
At the beginning of the ending
Do I stare or blink?

POTENTIALLY ANYWAY

Potentially, anyway, there is more
to the presence of the tree limb crews
on our street than the way they're cutting
around the wires and sapping the trees
with their uninspired angling. To be sure,

I am not thinking. I am looking, seriously

and deeply in invisible ways at invisible things—
the circulatory systems of the men
with their saws and the blood going around inside
a closed system—and in visible ways
at visible ones—the squirrels with green

berries and the robins on the awnings—and

it occurs to me in this moment that none of them are
thinking, for example, about mitochondria. I mean,
I don't know that for certain, but I can be pretty
certain—or certain enough—and it's obvious
that none of them are looking at me looking

at their hearts beating palpably, the men

and the squirrels and the robins now flown
from the awnings and onto the mailboxes

with the red flags up. Mail is outgoing as the air
in my lungs. How did I drift into this? Potentially,
anyway, I sat up and noticed more than wind

in the trees, and I knew it meant something

sentimental to me, because everything is
if one sees it that way, and I do see it that way,
because that is how I'm wired in the middle
of a life, for better and worse. And yes, I am okay,
and I am not okay both—thanks for asking—

but I do, when I can, wish to overflow and bury

myself in the azaleas of the next world.
Right now, however, I am somewhat content
to feel that the other beings I'm watching
are also feeling things. Some of them are
conscious of this and others probably not,

but everything that moves moves wisely

if you watch, or if you see it that way.
There is something inside us that shows
through our motion. I don't know for certain,
but I feel pretty sure, or I want to anyway.
Sentimental, I squint until my eyes become

stars, potentially or possibly, I can feel it.

DEAR BERSERKER

The light came into my dream
from the right, so I opened my eyes
to a mulberry bicycle that Sam stole
heavenward in a poem of many errors.
Then I was puffed rice or a poisonous
enjambment. I ate a bowl of scrambled eggs.
I could've sworn I was drowning in the engines
of an airport. Patiently, I contrived
to replace the painted target
with a small silver policeman,
redacted from the force. But
all of that was earlier, before I drove
Agnes and Juliet to their final exams
in Algebra and Chemistry, and also
before I went back to blitzing in the denim
and dimming—sitting for my portrait
in the juice of a lemon. Sometimes
more than one of them puckers
a Venus Flytrap or rattles a contingent
of cloches that stream from the Exits to enter
the drag-strip, the testicle, the syrup
of The Muses. Why The Fates
and The Hours often fail to intervene
is a question. Why The Sirens often fail
to alert me to their presence is another.
I'm already dead when I notice the petunia.

This particular occasion is whatever/wherever
you want it to be, or merely the time I have left
before I go to meet Dean and drink more
of the oracular in the future where I'm shards
in the maw of the racehorse Conundrum. To start
or not to start? To stop or not to go? One thing
I can recommend is Andrei Voznesensky
via Anselm Hollo, where I, too, am hollow
and translated into a speakeasy, though
nothing's ever easy that involves language,
and just to be clear, this is not
"channel surfing," so don't believe
the one-trick readers of ponies.
I have never been a pony, and this isn't
some trick, it's a real fucking miracle.
If you can't see the ineffable in the shattered
geraniums of saints, then you have problems
that I can't even begin to address.
Let's just say we agree to split the baby birds
into teams—your failure of imagination
versus my deliberate distortions.
The long bombs get longer in the teeth
with every wallop. I've never met a shadow
in the light I didn't like. The score
is a touchdown on an alien planet.
I am the alien at home in my amazement,
and you're what comes in waves to destroy me.

A NATURAL ARDOR

When one animal bites another
on the neck it's usually not
a good sign for the animal
being bitten into, just like when
one company bites into another
by buying up all its stock
for a majority stake, so it can
bleed its competition and extend
its reach like a wire brush
up a nostril. Suddenly,
the Red Sea pours over the top
of Pharoah's army—that is, at least
figuratively in the Old Testament
which is all retribution and promises
to God's children. God is good
somebody says, but always
that goodness is complicated.
What all of this has to do with you
and me is, frankly, not clear yet.
What I do know is that,
after two days of being
stand-offish, Bear, my dog, finally ate
the food in his bowl.
He must've been hungry
since there are no baby gazelles
or chickens in our living room

running around for him to bite down on
with that wild look in his eyes
that he gets whenever anyone comes
to the door. Bear is a good dog
someone says—except when he's not
or on one of his hunger strikes
or loose running the neighborhood,
having escaped us. The prodigal dog
doesn't come when we call. So anything
with Bear is always complicated, but not
in the same way that God's goodness
is complicated. I was talking about this
with my daughter, Agnes, when
she received the good news
that she got a full-tuition scholarship
to Ohio University and admittance
to their Honors College. Congratulations
Agnes! But she will turn it down, she tells us
later—with a lot of pomp and circumstance—
because OU's in a rather isolated small town
in Southeastern, Ohio, and she wants to study
Art History in a big city. She thinks
the prestige of the school she ultimately chooses
and whether it's situated in a hard-hearted metropolis
near Artworld-type people and museums galore
will make a massive difference
both now and in the future,
even though we know it doesn't really matter
where you get your undergraduate degree, nor

really what you study, unless
you're trying to learn to take a giant bite
out of someone else's neck. Things aren't
always so cut and dry or dog eat dog
or god eat god, or, maybe they are, or
at least more so than we'd like to admit
when the world is always clamping down
its fangs on the meek. They shall not
inherit the earth, very clearly. Inheritance,
in economic terms, is a privilege
of the rich, and we are not that. But
we aren't meek either, so
what difference does it make
one way or the other? Clearly,
we're in the middle of something,
but it feels like the end. And God is not
good. Or maybe everything isn't always
a matter of good and bad or right and wrong,
black and white or opaque and transparent.
Maybe God's irrelevant. Or God's a good dog.
Or God is dead meat with a wild
gamey look, biting down hard
on a part of us that's soft.

MEANINGFULNESS

Again the music stops—
the end of an a/side—so I wake up
and turn the record over, then go back
to thinking about the large

and scraggly coyote I saw last night
standing on the edge of Mount Airy Forest.
Does a forest technically have an edge?
I certainly have an edge and technically

have rubbed people the wrong way with it
as if polishing a tarnished lamp or
a brackish sky with a blueberry.
Never, though, have I been granted

three wishes by a lamp's genie, but
if I did, I would wish for food, shelter, and
healthcare for everyone,
so that we could upend capitalism and

begin to roll around in the moon's silver
nakedness for its own sake
and thus become reacquainted
with beauty's impossible possibilities.

But this is not about that.
This is about something germane
to the way the world is
rather than the way it might be.

The coyote on the edge of the forest
looked serious. So now I am trying out
being serious in imitation
of its wildness. And in that spirit,

I've broken my hand merely swinging
a golf club, which is really just a symptom
of a much larger brokenness
I walk around with all the time,

like the brokenness of a béchamel
or a volouté or my sense of French
grammar, the violets and variables
and maggots on the garbage

that weren't there yesterday, but
somehow have materialized
to remind me of myself. Maybe
that coyote was just staring

into space or watching the cars pass,
thinking human beings are too fast
for love, but not like a heavy metal record,
more like the way the urgency

to produce content and achieve things
keeps us from ourselves, so off
in the distance still trying to understand
how to live and what to do, but

always—or almost always— failing.
What I keep returning to lately, apropos
of almost nothing, is what I imagine
as the day I was born, how weird

I probably was in my wet suit of blood.
The promise of life is an ending
that forms while time speeds by
and a coyote looks on,

and for almost half a second
there's a meaning.

CAMELLIA

No more teaching people how to live
and what to do. Today's a star, or
I am searching for the endless
endlessness inside myself. And in yourself
a flowering disco ball of folding
chairs clanging against my rather boney exterior.
Also, in case you may know something, I'm looking
for a non-alcoholic beer that actually tastes
like it's drunk. I know I make it weirder
when I stare, so I don't look much
like I used to in store windows
or on the spines of books
with a blankness. No wonder
I can't find anything to drink. Water water
everywhere... And there's a bleakness
to this unprocessed process, which is
every day until never again. Sooner
than later I will wash up with you
on a shore somewhere, tangled in kelp
and old plastic bags, battered
by a shopping cart of bad clams,
probably littlenecks or razors.
If you've ever had a bad clam,
you know the end result, but if you haven't
you've at least read Emily Dickinson,
so Death is just dead or dying and also

the speaker of this poem. I bet
you weren't aware of that until now,
and it definitely changes everything.
You may want to go back
to the beginning to really suss it out,
or maybe you're like me
and just think, nah, I've had enough.
That should be the end, but I'm pretty
sure it's not. There will be hell
to pay eventually for the disorder
of your arrangements. But hey,
I'm just the messenger and guide
to the mysteries, the hysterics, the infinite
applause. As in life, here, you're on your own.
Smell you later. Not really. Way to go.
The eagle will escort you to your rock.

THE SHADOW OF THE EAGLE

No one's heart is in my ear.
I clock what works, so the blur
begins to thud. WTF? The eagle
flies over us, but I'm the only one
who notices it, because I'm always looking up
when everyone else is a baby or a puppy
tethered to the big fat milk of the earth.
Some wear blue dresses. Others
wear bows. A few just have fur
growing out of their ears. I grab an apple
from the fridge, and I crunch it
with my teeth. I crunch it into sauce
with a ravenous invective. I run my hands
through the galaxy of my hair, and the air
feels soft as a bunny or a drunk.
You know the kind I mean
always getting snared
in the lawnmower's blades.
I've never been sorrier than I am
when that happens, though
for the record it's never happened
to me. So what I'm saying is
I've never been sorrier
          no one's heart is in my ear,
but someone is a throwback
to an earlier tradition,

which means they don't have the right
relationship to history
in the present being now
and then later in a bubble of what was.
Here in this instant
I am rummaging the gauze,
but not in it. I am interested
in the ones who make
the wildest lunges at the sea
or into space. The wound
is too deep to go into
a poem. You should see
the look on your face
when you read that. What you're feeling
can't be particularly stated
in the didactic, but it has something
in common with a profusion
of doves. The shadow of the eagle
never fades, but it passes
eventually. The shadow of the eagle.
The shadow of the eagle.
The shadow of the eagle.

AESTHETICITY

My back is too rubble
to pay for the gas.
My heartache is lost
on a pretzel bun Reuben.
And everyone explodes
into letters that flutter,
but some of them never
get read or even opened,
so the call doesn't receive
a response from the tower.
The pass is incomplete.
The end zone is quiet.
I feel the breakfast grass
on my feet where I hover.
My toes are pink piglets
that squeal when I step on them.
In wildness is the preservation.
The fuck is the opera.
The stars open their mouths,
but I object to their subjects.
It is too dark in America
for nuclear fusion
going on and on and on
around the edges.
The broken enjambments.
The hinges of jaws.

Alas, there is an imperative,
but no one makes it out.
Do some stretches.
Wave at the awe,
or wave at the wave
rushing up to your swingset.
Alive and inarticulate
in the neoprene spring,
I cough up the spreadsheet
and it spreads like a hound.
The prophet takes the word
and goes hungry.

SHEPHERD'S PIE

All of us, unraveled,
on a park bench eventually.
Maybe. But that shadow's for later.
Right now, there's a sheep
in my hair, a galaxy in my shoes.
It's an echo of New York,
so to open. Meanwhile,
my friends come and go
wondering what art still is
and ever was or might be.
We think it's a process
of resurrecting every day
to be a new version
of whatever we are.
We go for a beer, but
it's not as easy as it once was.
Now it's all experimental. It's four
small beers and we get to taste
each one and vote for the one
we want to taste forever.
But nothing tastes forever.
Nothing stands the test of rhyme,
especially a bad one, which is also
a pun. Everything goes bye-bye.
Even yon ancient mariner.
"Sorry, my man, I've a wedding to get to—"

As for taste, I've never understood
taste in the aesthetic sense,
which is obvious. Always drawn
to the gaudy, noisy, messed-up oblivious.
I vote for the beer that's the most
inexplicable. I vote for the park bench
with the broken back leg,
the overlapping tags of graffiti to read.
Then I go to see some paintings,
but all they are is music,
which I decide on the spot is a bonus.
One of my friends needs urgent care,
so I take him and he's afraid.
I am also afraid. I am always afraid.
But the sheep don't notice
my dark matter shoes,
the laces untied so I'm tripping.
And still I'm on the lookout,
guarding my loves. It's always
the same, and it's always
something different. I sit
on the high corner
of the park bench broken
and tie the loose ends
temporarily.

NIGHT MACHINE

The rabbit's small body is stretched out
just so. And some Styrofoam against it.
Like a person's on a gurney with a sheet draped
against it. Inexactly against it. You think

a cat must've gotten it, or a hawk, but then
abandoned it. A truck came up fast or a boom
in the distance. Fireworks or thunder
or so you imagine it, as I imagine you

to try and be objective, since I and you
are one and the same, always one
and the same, and the sky above the rabbit—a sky
which is blue or will be when the sun's up.

You are walking your dog, and the rabbit is all ready.
The rabbit is already. And you are thinking again
about the last days of your friend.
Ever truculent. Un- or im-prescribable.

What the world meant to him was invisible
with longing and something elser, something
divergent, divagated, chaotic at random.
Free-flowing between a rabbit and a person,

a tiny astronaut, a burning tree,
a cloudbank's fluid motion or a popsicle. Melting.
The small and the bedraggled. The known
and what will never. It's okay, you think,

to feel unsettled about how to feel
and to wonder what your role was
in the countdown of his days.
It isn't always clear what a friendship entails

and what's involved in it both logically
and morally. Perhaps it seems odd
or out of place not to say emotionally
and generously. Or something. There are signs

behind the signposts and scenes behind the scenery.
Oxeye daisies, waving grain, grass mostly
carrying his voice into space. You are walking
your dog when you happen upon the rabbit.

And you imagine it sitting somewhere
just yesterday quiet, still yet animated,
its nose in small circles, its heart beating faster.
Faster than your own ever has or will you think.

But the world or time or nature intervened
to stop what could've and might've possibly
gone on. There is nothing you could've done.
Everything was arranged. Or

it only merely happened. The rabbit's light
shadow crosses the street. Your friend's wild
voice in your mouth when you speak.

PERSONAL POEM #11

"Matt, it's Dean, I'm here!" —Dean Young

It's 4:31PM in Westwood, and my ears
are wildly ringing on New Year's Eve,
because I just spent the last hour
and a half listening to Dean's last voice
message to me, which was his first
in Cincinnati, frazzled and looking

                          for a beer

The ringing is because I was playing it
entirely too loud through a 12" Celestion
Creamback speaker connected to a Solid State
Fender Bassman FR1000 from 1969,
the year I was born, the year Americans
first kicked up dust on the moon
to make it weirder

                  Dean was fourteen,
and the astronauts were adults, and
I was a baby without words, which is still
how I sometimes think of myself, even though
I'm 53 and I now know a lot of words, including
"lexical" and "aesthete" and "antithesis" and "brool"
I'm not ashamed to say   I cry a lot

                     Apparently,
I have a new credit card offer in my email,
which I will ignore, and Rose Zinnia doesn't

have a copy of my new book yet, which
I will attend to   I never imagined
that Dean would be gone into particles
and waves just like that at the age of 67,
or that I would be writing back and forth
in the dark with Mark about poetry
and Hüsker Dü and my diabetic terror
                              Whatever
is going to happen is already happening
is something Ted Berrigan took from
Alfred North Whitehead's metaphysics
but how my repeating it is connected
to what came before it, or now after it, i.e.
the fact that today Mel can't shake her dream
from last night where Bear bit her
on the finger, even though he's our dog
and soft and has never bitten anyone,
is beyond me   Suddenly
                     I'm also kind of excited
to be cognizant of the fact (though again
I'm not sure why it's occurring to me this instant)
that it's not at all improbable that the Bengals will go
to The Super Bowl for the second year in a row
Football is serious   Dreams are scary or hilarious
or both   Mark will no doubt think
there's a randomness to all of this, but let's hear it
for Joe Burrow and love   Let's remember Dean
falling into the Christmas tree last Christmas—
his last Christmas ever—at 3127 Manning Ave.

Let's consider
this meandering recklessness
a walk in the footsteps of the giants of the art
and a description of me trying to reckon
with a ghost—his voice on a loop
getting beer like a bell   This year
I won't lose anyone

ACKNOWLEDGMENTS

Thank you to the editors of the following publications where some of the poems in the "New Poems" section of this book first appeared: *The American Poetry Review, The Brooklyn Rail, Coma, Hamilton Stone Review, New Ohio Review, Oxeye*, and *Poetry*.

Thank you to Angela Ball for including "Dear Berserker" in her "New York School Diaspora" column at *The Best American Poetry Blog* and to Chris Mattingly and Laurel Leonetti, the editors of alla testa press, for including some of these poems in the chapbooks, *Dailiness* and *The Lyrical Ballads*.

Thank you to the Ohio Arts Council for a generous 2024 Individual Excellence Award in Poetry, which afforded me the time to assemble this behemoth (and two other manuscripts!), but also to write new poems, read, and think.

I am wildly grateful to Eric Appleby for the book's interior design and to Rose Zinnia for the cover design, but also to both of them for their endless patience with my numerous requests for changes, edits, noodle-y tweaks, and general demolition work.

Dobby Gibson (who, after all these years, remains burgled by dusk) read an early version of *FALLING FINE* and was indispensable in helping me select (and deselect) work from the previous books. Thank you, friend.

Sadly, there isn't space here to constellate all the other names of the dear small press/poetry friends in my community, but you know who you are, and I'm grateful to every one of you. Big love.

Biggest love of all to Melanie and Agnes Hart, without whom I would burst into flames.

Additional thanks go to my students, former students, and colleagues at the Art Academy of Cincinnati and in the Pacific Northwest College of Art/Willamette University Low-Res MFA Program.

Finally, HUGE THANKS to the small presses and editors I've worked with over the years, who published the books in which the selected poems originally appeared. Most especially on this front, I want to thank Dave Torneo at Pickpocket Books, who has been unwavering in his kindness, patience, and generosity— both of spirit and with his (pick)pocketbook.

This book is dedicated to the memory of Dean Young, my now invisible mentor. Thank you, friend. Rave on!

ABOUT THE AUTHOR

MATT HART is the author of twelve previous books of poetry, including most recently *FAMILIAR* (also from Pickpocket Books). He was a co-founder and the editor-in-chief of *Forklift, Ohio: A Journal of Poetry, Cooking, & Light Industrial Safety* from 1993-2019. The Head of Creative Writing at the Art Academy of Cincinnati, and a faculty mentor in the PNCA/Willamette University Low-Residency MFA Program, he lives in Cincinnati where he plays in the post-punk/indie rock band NEVERNEW and edits, solders, and publishes the journal *SOLID STATE.*